2nd Workshop on Natural Language Processing and Linked Open Data 2015 (NLP&LOD2)

International Conference on Recent Advances in Natural Language Processing 2015

Hissar, Bulgaria
11 September 2015

ISBN: 978-1-5108-1783-8

Printed from e-media with permission by:

Curran Associates, Inc.
57 Morehouse Lane
Red Hook, NY 12571

proceedings.com

Some format issues inherent in the e-media version may also appear in this print version.

Printed by Curran Associates, Inc. (2015)

For permission requests, please contact the Association for Computational Linguistics
at the address below.

Association for Computational Linguistics
209 N. Eighth Street
Stroudsburg, Pennsylvania 18360

Phone: 1-570-476-8006
Fax: 1-570-476-0860

acl@aclweb.org

Additional copies of this publication are available from:

Curran Associates, Inc.
57 Morehouse Lane
Red Hook, NY 12571 USA
Phone: 845-758-0400
Fax: 845-758-2634
Email: curran@proceedings.com
Web: www.proceedings.com

Introduction

NLP started to use extensively LOD in various scenarios, such as: exploring knowledge datasets (DBPedia, FreeBase, GeoNames, etc.) for annotation and information extraction; publishing language resources as LOD (WordNet, FrameNet, etc.); aggregating of the available data for various tasks (BabelNet, Global WordNet Grid); creation of standards for LOD (LEMON); building ontologies for different domains.

At the same time, the NLP processing pipelines have been developed towards the recognition and extraction of entities and events from raw stream data. Handling of events, however, requires also the inclusion of high quality modules like NER, NED, Semantic Role Labeling (SRL), sense and valency annotation. These modules rely not only on canonical resources, but also on the LOD datasets for extracting information about people, facts, and organizations. Additionally NLP techniques are used for creation of LOD datasets on the basis of new textual information.

Since there is some experience gained now in the interaction between NLP and LOD as well as between LOD and NLP, some problems have been identified, too. These are: general failure of NLP technology to meet completely the requirements of LOD; incompleteness of LOD datasets; sparseness of LOD datasets through various languages and domains; lack of robust reasoning mechanisms in NLP and LOD; still inefficient handling of natural language non-literal phenomena, such as metonymy, polysemy, figurative expressions; usability and re-usability of NLP and LOD applications.

Thus, a number of issues are related to the interaction between NLP and LOD. These are: reasons for low precision and inconsistencies; enhancing NLP applications with LOD; information extraction from LOD using NLP techniques; manipulating LOD (cleaning, adding information, deleting information, reconstructing facts) with NLP techniques; LOD as a corpus; mapping LOD to common sense ontologies and language data; storing LOD in RDF bases; methodological and theoretical approaches to LOD; handling polysemy and metonymy of entities in LOD; incompleteness of LOD data; LOD as unbalanced data through countries, cultures and topics of interest; insufficient reasoning in NLP and LOD; dynamics of LOD and NLP: versioning, replication, provenance, etc.

There are 6 papers accepted at the workshop. They cover the following topics: resources for Linked Open Data; representation of language phenomena in Linked Open Data; unified access to Linked Open Data and an ontology-based POS tagger using unifications of different tagsets.

We wish you a pleasant reading!

The Organizers

Organizers:

Piek Vossen, VU University Amsterdam
German Rigau, University of the Basque Country
Petya Osenova, Sofia University, Bulgaria
Kiril Simov, Bulgarian Academy of Sciences, Bulgaria

Program Committee:

Eneko Agirre, University of the Basque Country, Spain
Kalina Boncheva, Sheffield University, UK
António Branco, University of Lisbon, Portugal
Aljoscha Burchardt, DFKI, Germany
Nicoletta Calzolari, Istituto di Linguistica Computazionale, Italy
Philipp Cimiano, University of Bielefeld, Germany
Christian Chiarcos, Goethe-University Frankfurt am Main, Germany
Thierry Declerck, DFKI, Germany
Markus Egg, Humboldt-University Berlin, Germany
Jan Hajič, Charles University in Prague, Czech Republic
John McCrae, University of Bielefeld, Germany
Petya Osenova, Sofia University and IICT-BAS, Bulgaria
Maciej Piasecki, Wroclaw University of Technology, Poland
German Rigau, University of the Basque Country, Spain
Felix Sasaki, DFKI, Germany
Kiril Simov, IICT-BAS, Bulgaria
Gertjan van Noord, University of Groningen, The Netherlands
Piek Vossen, Vrije Universiteit Amsterdam, The Netherlands

Invited Speaker:

German Rigau, University of the Basque Country

Table of Contents

Workshop Program

09:00–09:30 ***Welcome***

Invited lecture

09:30–10:30 *Cross-lingual Event Detection in Discourse*
German Rigau

Session 1:

10:30–11:00 *Generating Lexicalization Patterns for Linked Open Data*
Rivindu Perera and Parma Nand

11:00–11:30 **Coffee break**

Session 2:

11:30–12:00 *Small in Size, Big in Precision: A Case for Using Language-Specific Lexical Resources for Word Sense Disambiguation*
Steven Neale, João Silva and António Branco

12:00–12:30 *Towards the Representation of Hashtags in Linguistic Linked Open Data Format*
Thierry Declerck and Piroska Lendvai

12:30–14:00 **Lunch break**

Session 3:

14:00–14:30 *An Ontology-based Approach To Automatic Part-of-Speech Tagging Using Heterogeneously Annotated Corpora*
Maria Sukhareva and Christian Chiarcos

14:30–15:00 *Accessing Linked Open Data via A Common Ontology*
Kiril Simov and Atanas Kiryakov

15:00–15:30 *The GuanXi network: a new multilingual LLOD for Language Learning applications*
Ismail El Maarouf, Hatem Mousselly Sergieh, Eugene Alferov, Haofen Wang, Zhijia Fang and Doug Cooper

15:30–16:00 **Discussion and Closing**

Cross-lingual Event Detection in Discourse

German Rigau
Computer Science Faculty, EHU
german.rigau@ehu.eus

Abstract

We describe a system for event extraction across documents and languages. We developed a framework for the interoperable semantic interpretation of mentions of events, participants, locations and time, as well as the relations between them.

Furthermore, we use a common RDF model to represent instances of events and normalised entities and dates. We convert multiple mentions of the same event in English and Spanish to a single representation. We thus resolve cross-document event and entity coreference within a language but also across languages. We tested our system on a Wikinews corpus of 120 English articles that have been manually translated to Spanish.

We report on the cross-lingual cross-document event and entity extraction comparing the Spanish output with respect to English.

1 Speaker's Bio

German Rigau Ph.D. and B.A. in Computer Science by the Universitat Politecnica de Catalunya (UPC). Formerly member of the Computer Science department at the UPC and member of the TALP research group of the UPC, currently, he is teaching at the Computer Science Faculty of the EHU as an Associate Professor. He has published more than hundred-refereed articles and conference papers in the area of Natural Language Processing, and in particular Acquisition of Lexical Knowledge, Word Sense Disambiguation, Semantic Processing and Inferencing.

He has been involved in several European research projects (ESPRIT BRA ACQUILEX, ACQUILEX II, LE EUROWORDNET, LE NAMIC, MEANING, KYOTO, PATHS, OpeNER and NewsReader). He coordinated the 5th Framework MEANING project (IST-2001-34460) and the local groups for NAMIC, KYOTO and OpeNER. Currently, he is coordinating the local group for NewsReader (FP7-ICT-2011-8-316404).

He has been also involved in several Spanish National research projects (ITEM, HERMES, SENSEM, KNOW, KNOW2 and SKaTer). Currently, he is coordinating the local group of the SKaTer project. He served as PC member and reviewer of the main international conferences and workshops in NLP and AI including ACL, EACL, NAACL, COLING, AAAI, ECAI, IJCAI, EMNLP, IJCNLP, CoNLL, TSD, SENSEVAL/SEMEVAL and IWC.

He also served as reviewer of International Journals including: Computers and the Humanities, Journal of Natural Language Engineering, Journal of Artificial Intelligence Research and Artificial Intelligence. He has also participated in all editions of the international competition of SENSEVAL.

Currently, he is member of the Association for Computational Linguistics (ACL) and the Spanish Society for Natural Language Processing (SEPLN).

Proceedings of the Second Workshop on Natural Language Processing and Linked Open Data, page 1,
Hissar, Bulgaria, 11 September 2015.

Generating Lexicalization Patterns for Linked Open Data

Rivindu Perera and **Parma Nand**
Auckland University of Technology
Auckland, New Zealand
{rperera, pnand}@aut.ac.nz

Abstract

The concept of Linked Data has attracted increased interest in recent times due to its free and open availability and the sheer of volume. We present a framework to generate patterns which can be used to lexicalize Linked Data. We use DBpedia as the Linked Data resource which is one of the most comprehensive and fastest growing Linked Data resource available for free. The framework incorporates a text preparation module which collects and prepares the text after which Open Information Extraction is employed to extract relations which are then aligned with triples to identify patterns. The framework also uses lexical semantic resources to mine patterns utilizing VerbNet and WordNet. The framework achieved 70.36% accuracy and a Mean reciprocal Rank value of 0.72 for five DBpedia ontology classes generating 101 lexicalizations.

1 Introduction

Semantic web continues to grow rapidly in various forms. Two key areas that recent semantic web researches have focused on are enrichment of Linked Data resources and using these resources in different applications.

DBpedia, Freebase, and YAGO[1] are frontiers in Linked Data area. The Linked Data is represented as triples (a data structure in the form of ⟨subject, predicate, object⟩) using Resource Description Framework (RDF). As Linked Data concept moves forward, there is also a need to utilize this data in applications. A major area that requires Linked Data is Natural Language Processing (NLP) and applications such as Question Answering (QA) (Perera, 2012a; Perera, 2012b). A drawback of Linked Data is that it lacks the linguistic information which can be used to turn them back to a natural textual format.

Generating linguistic structures and choosing words to communicate a particular abstract representation (e.g., triple) is referred to as lexicalization which is a subtask in Natural Language Generation. The work described in this paper is a part of our NLG project[2] currently under way (Perera and Nand, 2014a; Perera and Nand, 2014b; Perera and Nand, 2014c). The framework presented in this paper uses DBpedia as the Linked Data resource and lexicalization is presented as the mining best available pattern to generate a natural language representation for the triple being considered.

The remainder of the paper is structured as follows. Section 2 presents related work in the area of lexicalization. In Section 3 we describe the proposed framework in detail. Section 4 presents the experiments used to validate the framework. Section 5 concludes the paper with an outlook on future work.

2 Related work

Duma and Klein (2013) present an approach to extract templates to verbalize triples using a heuristic. The main drawbacks noticed in this model are the ignorance of additional textual resources and less consideration on the cohesive pattern generation

Lemon model (Walter et al., 2013) extracts lexicalizations for DBpedia using dependency patterns extracted from Wikipedia sentences. However, the initial experiments we performed have shown that this approach fails completely when provided with sentences with grammatical conjunctions.

Ell and Harth (2014) introduce the language in-

[1] dbpedia.org, freebase.com, mpi-inf.mpg.de/yago/

[2] http://rivinduperera.com/information/realtextlex

Proceedings of the Second Workshop on Natural Language Processing and Linked Open Data, pages 2–5,
Hissar, Bulgaria, 11 September 2015.

dependent approach to generate RDF verbalization templates. This model utilizes the maximal sub-graph pattern extraction model. However, in our approach the Open Information Extraction (OpenIE) is utilized to get more coherent lexicalization patterns (Perera and Nand, 2015a; Perera and Nand, 2015b).

3 RealText$_{lex}$ framework

Fig. 1 depicts the high-level overview of the process of generating lexicalization patterns in the proposed framework. The process starts with a given DBpedia ontology class (e.g., person, organization, etc.). The following sections explains the process in detail.

3.1 Candidate sentence extraction

The objective of candidate sentence extractor is to identify potential sentences that can lexicalize a given triple. The input is taken as a collection of co-reference resolved sentences and a set of triples. This unit firstly verbalizes the triples using a set of rules. Then each sentence is analysed to check either complete subject (s), the object (o) or the predicate (p) are mentioned in the sentence (S). This sentence analysis assigns a score to each sentence based on presence of a triple. The score is the ratio of subject, predicate and object present in the sentence.

3.2 Open Information Extraction

Once the candidate sentences are selected for each triple, we then extract relations from these candidate sentences employing Open IE. The Open IE (Etzioni et al., 2008) essentially focuses on domain independent relation extraction and predominantly targets the web as a corpus for deriving the relations. The framework proposed in this paper uses textual content extracted from the web which works with a diverse set of domains. Specifically, the framework uses Ollie Open IE system[3] for relation extraction. This module associates each relation with the triple and outputs a triple-relations collection. A relation is composed of first argument (arg1), relation (rel), and second argument (arg2).

3.3 Pattern processing and combination

This module generates patterns from aligned relations in Section 3.2. In addition to these patterns, verb frame based patterns are also determined and added to the pattern list.

3.3.1 Relation based patterns

Based on the aligned relations and triples, a string based pattern is generated. These string based patterns can get two forms as shown in Fig. 2 for two sample scenarios. The subject and object are denoted by symbols *s?* and *o?* respectively.

3.3.2 Verb frame based patterns

The framework utilizes two lexical semantic resources, VerbNet and WordNet to mine patterns. Currently, the framework generates only one type of pattern (`s? Verb o?`), if the predicate is a verb and if that verb has the frame {*Noun phrase, Verb, Noun phrase*} in either VerbNet or WordNet.

3.3.3 Property based patterns

The predicates which cannot be associated with a pattern in the above processes described in Section 3.3.1 and Section 3.3.2 are properties belonging to the DBpedia resources selected. The left over predicates are assigned a generic pattern (`s? has ⟨predicate⟩ of o?`) based on the specific predicate.

3.4 Pattern enrichment

Pattern enrichment adds two types of additional information; grammatical gender related to the pattern and multiplicity level associated with the determined pattern. When searching a pattern in the lexicalization pattern database, these additional information is also mined in the lexicalization patterns for a given predicate of an ontology class.

3.4.1 Grammatical gender determination

The lexicalization patterns can be accurately reused later only if the grammatical gender is recorded with the pattern. For example, consider triple, ⟨`Walt Disney, spouse, Lillian Disney`⟩ and lexicalization pattern, "`s? is the husband of o?`". This pattern cannot be reused to lexicalize the triple ⟨`Lillian Disney, spouse, Walt Disney`⟩, because the grammatical gender of the subject is now different, even though the property (spouse) is same in both scenarios. The framework uses three types of grammatical gender types (male, female, neutral) based on the triple subject and it is determined by DBpedia grammatical gender dataset (Mendes et al., 2012).

[3]knowitall.github.io/ollie/

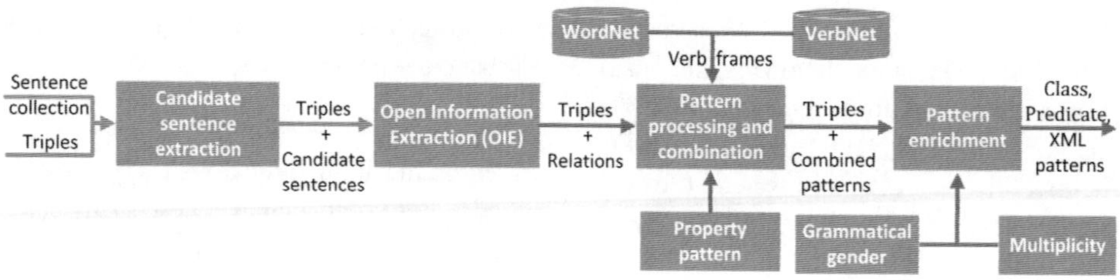

Figure 1: Schematic representation of the complete framework

- ⟨Walt Disney, birth date, 1901-12-05⟩
  - `arg1:` Walt Disney, `rel:` was born on, `arg2:` December 5, 1901 `pattern:` s? was born on o?
- ⟨Walt Disney, designer, Mickey Mouse⟩
  - `arg1:` Mickey Mouse, `rel:` is designed by, `arg2:` Walt Disney `pattern:` o? is designed by s?

Figure 2: Basic patterns generated for two sample triples. *s?* and *o?* represent subject and object respectively.

3.4.2 Multiplicity determination

In DBpedia page for Nile River has three countries listed under the predicate "country" because it does not belong to one country, but flows through these countries. However, East River belongs only to United States. The lexicalization patterns generated for these two scenarios will also be different and cannot be shared. For example, lexicalization pattern for Nile river will in the form of "`s? flows through o?`" and for East River it will be like "`s? is in o?`". To address this variation, our framework checks whether there are multiple object values for the same subject and predicate, then it adds the appropriate property value (multiple/single) to the pattern.

4 Experimental framework

4.1 Experimental settings and results

Table 1 shows the summary of the breakdown of the results for pattern extraction. The last 5 columns of the table also shows the results for the pattern enrichment modules. To get a clear idea on the accuracy of the framework, we checked how many syntactically correct lexicalization patterns appear as the highest ranked pattern for the given predicate. In this context syntactic correctness was considered as being both grammatically accurate and coherent. The results of this evaluation is shown in Fig. 3 for each of the ontology classes.

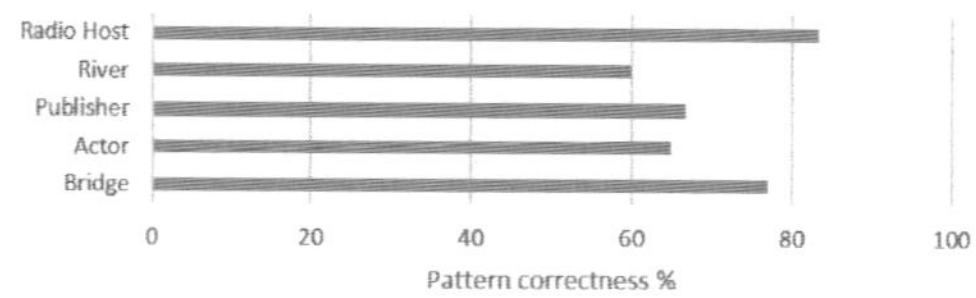

Figure 3: Analysis of syntactic correctness of the extracted patterns

Since, the framework ranks lexicalization patterns using a scoring system, we considered it as a method that provides a set of possible outputs. We decided to get a statistical measurement incorporating Mean Reciprocal Rank (MRR) as shown below to compute the rank of the first correct pattern of each predicate in each ontology class.

$$MRR = \frac{1}{|P|} \sum_{i=1}^{|P|} \frac{1}{rank_i} \quad (1)$$

where P and $rank_i$ represent predicates and the rank of the correct lexicalization for the ith predicate respectively. Table 2 depicts the MRR results for the 5 ontology classes being considered.

Table 3 shows a statistical summary of proposed approach.

4.2 Observations and discussions

The following observations can be made based on the results of the experiment. Fig. 3 shows that our framework has achieved 70.36% average accuracy for 5 ontology classes where the lowest accuracy was reported as 60%. This evaluation does not take into account the rank of the correct lexicalization patterns and measures the number of correct patterns present in the extracted set of patterns. On the other hand, MRR based evaluation

Table 1: Results of the pattern extraction module

Ontology class	Relational patterns	Frame patterns	Property patterns	Pattern enrichment				
				Multiplicity		Grammatical gender		
				Multiple	Single	Male	Female	Neutral
Bridge	272	8	9	163	126	0	0	289
Actor	422	0	16	369	69	400	22	16
Publisher	39	1	4	32	12	0	0	44
River	157	2	10	158	11	0	0	169
Radio Host	30	1	1	14	18	0	0	32

Table 2: Mean Reciprocal Rank analysis for ranked lexicalization patterns

	Bridge	Actor	Publish	River	Radio Host
MRR	0.77	0.69	0.72	0.61	0.83

Table 3: Statistics of evaluation of proposed approach

Candidate templates	Lexicalizations	Accuracy
393	101	70.36%

provides an detailed look at ranking of the first correct lexicalization. Average MRR value of 0.724 achieved for 5 ontology classes. Finally, based on the comparison in Table 3, it is clear that proposed approach in this paper has advanced the way of deriving lexicalizations by generating reasonable number of valid patterns and with a higher accuracy.

5 Conclusion and future work

This paper presented a framework to generate lexicalization patterns for DBpedia triples using a pipeline of processes. The pipeline starts with ontology classes which is then used to mine patterns aligning triples with relations extracted from sentence collections from the web. The framework generated patterns were human-evaluated and showed an accuracy of 70.36% and a MRR of 0.72 on test dataset. In future, we aim to target on expanding the test collection to build a reasonable sized lexicalization pattern database for DBpedia.

References

Daniel Duma and Ewan Klein. 2013. Generating natural language from linked data: Unsupervised template extraction. In *IWCS-2013*.

Basil Ell and Andreas Harth. 2014. A language-independent method for the extraction of rdf verbalization templates. In *INLG-2014*.

Oren Etzioni, Michele Banko, Stephen Soderland, and Daniel S. Weld. 2008. Open information extraction from the web. *Communications of the ACM*, 51.

Pablo N. Mendes, Max Jakob, and Christian Bizer. 2012. DBpedia for NLP: A Multilingual Cross-domain Knowledge Base. In *LREC-2012*.

Rivindu Perera and Parma Nand. 2014a. Interaction history based answer formulation for question answering. In *KESW-2014*, pages 128–139.

Rivindu Perera and Parma Nand. 2014b. Real text-cs - corpus based domain independent content selection model. In *ICTAI-2014*, pages 599–606.

Rivindu Perera and Parma Nand. 2014c. The role of linked data in content selection. In *PRICAI-2014*, pages 573–586.

Rivindu Perera and Parma Nand. 2015a. A multi-strategy approach for lexicalizing linked open data. In *CICLing-2015*, pages 348–363.

Rivindu Perera and Parma Nand. 2015b. Realtext-lex: A lexicalization framework for linked open data. In *ISWC-2015 Demonstration*.

Rivindu Perera. 2012a. Ipedagogy: Question answering system based on web information clustering. In *T4E-2012*.

Rivindu Perera. 2012b. *Scholar: Cognitive Computing Approach for Question Answering*. Honours thesis, University of Westminster.

Sebastian Walter, Christina Unger, and Philipp Cimiano. 2013. A corpus-based approach for the induction of ontology lexica. In *NLDB-2013*, Salford.

Small in Size, Big in Precision: A Case for Using Language-Specific Lexical Resources for Word Sense Disambiguation

Steven Neale, João Silva and António Branco
Department of Informatics
Faculty of Sciences
University of Lisbon, Portugal
{steven.neale, jsilva, antonio.branco}@di.fc.ul.pt

Abstract

Linked open data (LOD) presents an ideal platform for connecting the multilingual lexical resources used in natural language processing (NLP) tasks, but the use of machine translation to fill in gaps in lexical coverage for resource-poor languages means that large amounts of data are potentially unverified. For graph-based word sense disambiguation (WSD), one approach has been to first translate terms into English in order to disambiguate using richer, fuller lexical knowledge bases (LKBs) such as WordNet.

In this paper, we show that this approach actually creates more ambiguity and is far less accurate than using language-specific resources, which, regardless of their smaller size, can provide results comparable in accuracy to the state-of-the-art reported for graph-based WSD *in* English. For LOD, this demonstrates the importance of continuing to grow and extend language-specific resources in order to continually verify and reintegrate them as accurate resources.

1 Introduction

In the context of natural language processing (NLP), word sense disambiguation (WSD) refers to the computational problem of determining the 'sense' or meaning of a word when used in a particular context (Agirre and Edmonds, 2006). To use a classic example, the word 'bank' could be interpreted in the sense of the financial institution or as the slope of land at the side of a river, depending on the context in which it is used. Target words are disambiguated based on their context (determined based on the words surrounding them), and the potential senses that they could relate to (Nóbrega and Pardo, 2014).

Linked Open Data (LOD) – the implementation of best practices ensuring that not just documents but the data within them are structured and interconnected on the web – is particularly useful in tying together the resources used for knowledge-based WSD, which leverages existing collections and indexes of potential senses to choose the most appropriate for a given target word (Agirre and Edmonds, 2006). WSD research has tended to derive knowledge bases from stand-alone dictionaries and ontologies such as WordNet, where nouns, verbs, adjectives and adverbs are stored as 'synsets' and linked by their semantic relations (Fellbaum, 1998). Recent projects such as BabelNet (Navigli and Ponzetto, 2012) are now focusing on integrating these resources with encyclopedic information and making the connected data available as LOD.

Our work focuses on Portuguese, for which specific work on WSD – particularly involving Portuguese knowledge resources – is still limited, and usually either focused on particular domain areas and applications or achieved by translating terms to English in order to disambiguate using English knowledge sources (Nóbrega and Pardo, 2014). While there are similarities between Portuguese and other languages for which more substantial lexical resources and WSD research are already available – French and Spanish, for example – there are still enough differences to motivate specific research in Portuguese. The sheer number of 'false friends' – similar words with very different meanings – between Portuguese and Spanish (Director General of Translation, 2006) demonstrates the necessity of having Portuguese-specific resources available for lexically-motivated tasks such as WSD.

This paper describes a comparison between two approaches to performing graph-based WSD

Proceedings of the Second Workshop on Natural Language Processing and Linked Open Data, pages 6–15,
Hissar, Bulgaria, 11 September 2015.

in Portuguese; 1) using the smaller, language-specific Portuguese MultiWordNet (MultiWordNet, nd) as the underlying lexical knowledge base (LKB) for the WSD, and 2) translating open-class words in the input text from Portuguese to English in order to run WSD using the much larger English WordNet as the underlying LKB. The contributions from our results are twofold:

- Performing graph-based WSD using a smaller, language-specific LKB (Portuguese MultiWordNet) provides better results than translating terms to English in order to run WSD using the much larger English WordNet.
- The results obtained when performing graph-based WSD using a small, language-specific LKB (such as the Portuguese MultiWordNet) are comparably accurate with state-of-the-art results previously reported for graph-based WSD in English using WordNet.

These contributions suggest that for LOD, relying on machine translation to fill in the lexical gaps between resource-rich and research-poor languages (as with BabelNet) must only be a stopgap measure, and that work to grow and extend local, language-specific lexical resources such as WordNets should continue so that verified, accurate data can be properly linked and reintegrated with existing LOD later for use in NLP tasks such as WSD.

We first explore some related work (Section 2), before describing an implementation of graph-based WSD for Portuguese (Section 3). Next, we present our evaluation of the two approaches to WSD in Portuguese, using a gold-standard, human-annotated corpus for comparison (Section 4). Finally, we discuss the possible ramifications of our findings in the context of LOD (Section 5), before presenting our conclusions (Section 6).

2 Related Work

2.1 Knowledge and graph-based WSD

While WSD has traditionally delivered its best results using supervised and unsupervised machine learning methods, domain-specific knowledge-based WSD can now perform as well or better than a more generic, supervised machine learning-based WSD approach (Agirre et al., 2009). For example, in the medical domain good results have been obtained in WSD tasks by creating an LKB from the Unified Medical Language System (UMLS) Metathesarurus, a collection of more than one million biomedical concepts and five million concept names (Stevenson et al., 2011; Preiss and Stevenson, 2013).

Progress in knowledge-based WSD has largely been driven by the development of graph-based disambiguation methods, as pioneered by a number of researchers (Navigli and Velardi, 2005; Mihalcea, 2005; Sinha and Mihalcea, 2007; Navigli and Lapata, 2007; Agirre and Soroa, 2008). Graph-based methods allow LKBs such as WordNets to be represented as weighted graphs, where word senses correspond to nodes and the relationships or dependencies between pairs of senses correspond to the edges between nodes. The strength of the edge between two nodes, corresponding to the relationship or dependency between two synsets, can then be calculated using semantic similarity measures such as the Lesk algorithm (Lesk, 1986).

For WSD tasks, graph-based representations of LKBs can then be used to choose the most likely sense of a word in a given context, based on the dependencies between nodes in the graph (Agirre and Soroa, 2009). Algorithms such as PageRank (Brin and Page, 1998) allow for the weights and probabilities of directed links between target words and words in their local context to be spread over the entirety of the graph (Agirre and Soroa, 2009). Nodes (senses) 'recommend' each other based on their own importance – with the importance of any given node being higher or lower depending on the importance of other nodes which recommend it – and then follow a 'random walk' over the rest of the graph based on the importance of the nodes to whose edges they are attached (Mihalcea, 2005; Agirre and Soroa, 2009).

At the end of this random walk, the probability of a random walk from the target word's node ending on any other node in the graph has been calculated, thus allowing the most appropriate sense of the target word to be detemined. By utilizing the full extent of the graph-based representation of the LKB in this way, the performance of WSD in general (non-specific) domains has been shown to improve, becoming almost as efficient as supervised learning-based methods in some tasks (Agirre et al., 2014).

2.2 Linked Open Data and aligned LKBs

In parallel to the growing use and adaptation of different types of LKBs in knowledge and graph-based WSD, the lexical resources on which these LKBs and WSD methods depend are becoming increasingly linked, interconnected and accessible. Projects like MultiWordNet (MultiWordNet, nd) and EuroWordNet (Vossen, 2004) are built around the idea of aligning and mapping the identifier codes of WordNet-style synsets to each other, and in many languages. For knowledge-based WSD, this connectivity makes multilingual and language-specific WSD tasks and workflows much simpler to construct.

Recent LOD projects such as DBpedia (Lehmann et al., 2012) and BabelNet (Navigli and Ponzetto, 2012) are now collecting data from encyclopedic sources such as Wikipedia to create large-scale, structured multilingual knowledge bases. BabelNet, in particular, integrates both lexical and encyclopedic resources – chiefly WordNet and Wikipedia – to create a 'wide-coverage, multilingual semantic network' of not only information and concepts but also the semantic relationships between them (Navigli and Ponzetto, 2012). Like DBpedia – which connects the extracted knowledge from 111 different language editions of Wikipedia (Lehmann et al., 2012) – BabelNet is also multilingual, using machine translation techniques to fill in the lexical gaps in resource-poor languages (Navigli and Ponzetto, 2012).

2.3 Current state of WSD in Portuguese

Portuguese-specific WSD has also followed the knowledge-based trend. Early work focused on the automatic generation of disambiguation rules based on representations of meaning in pre-annotated corpora (Specia et al., 2005), before exploring hybrid approaches that leverage the relationships between different knowledge sources to support such rules (Specia, 2006; Specia et al., 2007). More recent work has focused on graph-based methods, leveraging WordNets as LKBs (Nóbrega and Pardo, 2014). However, this work assumes that translating Portuguese terms into English and then querying the English WordNet is sufficient for representing most of the senses found in Portuguese texts.

Spanish, which shares a degree of similarity with Portuguese, has been more widely explored in the context of WSD. Agirre and Soroa (2009) evaluated their graph-based WSD algorithm using the Spanish WordNet of approximately 67,000 senses (Atserias et al., 2004) as their LKB. They obtained promising results that approach those reported using the supervised 'most frequent sense' (MFS) baseline system for the SemEval-2007 Task 09 dataset (Màrquez et al., 2007). More recently, graph-based WSD performed over Spanish Babelnet senses as the LKB was shown to improve over the MFS baseline in the Multilingual Word Sense Disambiguation task at SemEval-2013 (Navigli et al., 2013).

These results are encouraging for the case of Portuguese, demonstrating that knowledge-based WSD produces good results using LKBs specific to similar languages. For Portuguese, it would thus seem more appropriate to grow Portuguese-specific lexical resources and to link them with existing resources in other languages as LOD, than to rely either on translating the input words to be disambiguated, as in (Nóbrega and Pardo, 2014), or on filling the gaps in one language by translating from the fuller lexical resources of other languages, as in BabelNet (Navigli and Ponzetto, 2012).

3 Implementing Graph-Based WSD for Portuguese

For the evaluations described in this paper, we use UKB, a collection of tools and algorithms (Agirre and Soroa, 2009; Agirre et al., 2014) for performing graph-based WSD over a pre-existing knowledge base. We use UKB for two reasons:

- UKB includes tools for automatically creating graph-based representations of LKBs in WordNet-style formats.
- The algorithm used by UKB for performing WSD over the graph itself has been consistently shown to produce results in line with or above the state-of-the-art (Agirre and Soroa, 2009; Agirre et al., 2014).

For the purpose of our work, we are thus able to perform highly-efficient disambiguation over an accurate graph-based representation of our chosen LKBs, meaning that any differences in results can be confidently attributed to the quality of either the input texts that are being disambiguated or to the LKBs themselves.

UKB first accepts input texts in a 'context' format, where each sentence in a text is treated as an individual context containing the target word and all other open-class words (nouns, verbs, adjectives and adverbs) from the original sentence. This context file can be easily extracted and arranged from input texts pre-tagged with lemmas and part-of-speech (PoS) tags, which we produce using the LX-Suite (Branco and Silva, 2006), a collection of shallow processing tools for Portuguese.

UKB then performs WSD for each sentence in the context file, using a PageRank-based (Brin and Page, 1998) random walk to return the probability of each node (synset) in a given graph being semantically related to a target word, and returning the appropriate synset identifier for the most likely node. It is this use of the words surrounding a target word in the context file – which are also included as nodes in the graph and whose relevance thus affects the final decision on which sense to assign – that separates UKB from similar algorithms and consistently delivers state-of-the-art results (Agirre and Soroa, 2009; Agirre et al., 2014).

The graphs used for the evaluation in this paper were created, using the tools supplied with UKB, from two different source LKBs – the Portuguese MultiWordNet (MultiWordNet, nd) and version 3.0 of the Princeton English WordNet (Fellbaum, 1998). These LKBs are described in more detail in the following section.

4 Evaluation

This section describes our comparison of the assignment of word senses by a human annotator with the output of two options for performing graph-based WSD in Portuguese:

- UKB-based WSD over the Portuguese MultiWordNet.
- UKB-based WSD over the English WordNet (using terms automatically translated from Portuguese to English)

For UKB-based WSD over the Portuguese MultiWordNet, we create the required dictionary files and corresponding graph from approximately 19,700 verified synsets. Because the synset identifiers are mapped to the corresponding synsets in the English WordNet, we are able to make use of the semantic relations in the English WordNet when building the graph – although the dictionary used is small at 19,700, the fuller representation of semantic relations for English ensures that the computed similarity between Portuguese dictionary items is more reliable. Semantic relations between glosses in the English WordNet are also used when building the graph, which our own experimentation and previous reporting of results using UKB (Agirre and Soroa, 2009; Agirre et al., 2014) have both shown to result in more accurate WSD.

For UKB-based WSD over the English WordNet, we follow the model used by Nóbrega and Pardo (2014) of translating ambiguous terms into English and then disambiguating them using the English WordNet. In practice, this involves translating the context file from Portuguese to English after the input text is preprocessed and tagged using the shallow processing tools, so as to have translated not just the target words but also the surrounding open class words in each sentence. The translated context file is then disambiguated by UKB using a dictionary file and corresponding graph created from the English WordNet, comprising approximately 117,000 synsets.

We have not been able to use the WordReference API (WordReference.com, nd) that Nóbrega and Pardo (2014) used for translating from Portuguese to English, for which user access is no longer being granted. Instead, we have created our own tool for translating terms from the context file word-by-word using BabelNet. Each individual Portuguese word to be translated is given together with its part of speech to BabelNet, which returns the most appropriate 'BabelSynset' for that word.

BabelSynsets are constructed from linked information from a variety of sources in different languages (including Wikipedia (Wikipedia, nd), WordNet (Fellbaum, 1998), Wiktionary (Wiktionary, nd), Wikidata (Wikidata, nd), OmegaWiki (OmegaWiki, nd) and various others) with gaps in resource-poor languages filled using machine translation. Every BabelSynset contains a list of translations of its main sense in different languages, and each of the possible translations for the word in each language has a weighting or probability attached to it. From this, we choose the best weighted translation from the English options and use this as the translation for the original Portuguese word in the context file.

CINTIL	UKB + PT	UKB + EN Translations
Manually disambiguated	45,502	45,502
Automatically disambiguated	59,190	112,678
Manually *and* automatically disamb.	45,386	41,441
Same sense assigned	29,540	12,563
Precision	65.09	30.32
Recall	64.92	27.61
F1	65.00	28.90

Table 1: Comparison of the performance of UKB-based WSD over the Portuguese MultiWordNet and by translating terms to English to be run over the English WordNet.

4.1 Gold-Standard Test Corpus

The CINTIL International Corpus of Portuguese (Barreto et al., 2006) was chosen as the gold-standard for our evaluation. It comprises approximately 1 million tokens manually annotated with lemmas, part-of-speech, inflection, and named entities, which are compatible with the input and output formats of the tools in the LX-Suite. The corpus contains data from both written sources and transcriptions of spoken Portuguese – we have used the data from the written part, sourced mainly from newspaper articles and short novels and comprising approximately 700,000 tokens, of which 193,443 are open class words.

Word senses were manually chosen and assigned to open-class words by a team of human annotators using the LX-SenseAnnotator tool (Neale et al., 2015), a graphical user interface for assigning senses from WordNet-style lexicons to pre-tagged input texts. The lexicon from which annotators were able to choose senses was the same Portuguese MultiWordNet (approximately 19,700 verified synsets) used in the evaluation. Because annotators were only able to select from the words and synets present in the Portuguese MultiWordNet, not all of the open-class words in the corpus were able to be annotated.

4.2 Performance for Portuguese

Running the UKB algorithm over the manually disambiuated CINTIL corpus, we can see how well the two approaches – disambiguation using the smaller Portuguese MultiWordNet or translating words to English and then disambiguating using the much larger English WordNet – perform when compared with disambiguation by a human annotator. As described earlier in section 4, the mapping of synset identifiers between the Portuguese and English WordNets allows the same graph to be used in both approaches (built based on the semantic relations between English synsets coupled with the semantic relations between English glosses) - it is the sizes of the dictionary files that link words to synsets in the graph that greatly differ.

Table 1 shows that 45,502 of the 193,443 open class words have been manually disambiguated. When running UKB over the dictionary files and graph built from the Portuguese MultiWordNet, 45,386 of the manually disambiguated words are also automatically disambiguated, from a total of 59,190 tagged by the algorithm. Note that although annotators may have chosen *not* to disambiguate certain words if they felt that the senses presented to them by the Portuguese MultiWordNet did not convey the required meaning, the UKB algorithm will always assign something from the options available to it, choosing the most probable sense from those provided.

This explains the greater number of senses automatically disambiguated than manually disambiguated, but without manual disambiguation we have no measure of whether the additional automatic disambiguation was correct or not. Thus, we here define recall as the number of words with the same sense assigned by UKB *and* the human annotator, divided by the number of words manually disambiguated (45,502). The UKB-based WSD was able to assign the same sense to the word as was chosen by the annotator for 29,540 of the 45,386 words for which the same sense was assigned manually and automatically, giving a precision of 65.09% and recall of 64.92%.

When running UKB by automatically translating ambiguous Portuguese terms into English and then running them over the dictionary files and graph built from the English WordNet, performance is greatly affected. Despite vastly more words being tagged with an assigned sense by the algorithm – 112,678 – a lower number of the words that were manually disambiguated end up being tagged as well – 41,441. The UKB-based WSD was able to assign the same sense to the word as was chosen by the annotator for just 12,563 of these words, giving a precision of 30.32% and recall of 27.61%

Corpus	LKB	F1
Senseval-2	WN3.0	70.3
Senseval-3	WN3.0	65.3
Semeval-07 (FG)	WN3.0	56.0
Semeval-07 (CG)	WN3.0	83.6
CINTIL	PT MWN	65.0

Table 2: Comparison of UKB-based WSD over the Portuguese MultiWordNet with previously reported state-of-the-art results (for nouns).

Table 2 compares the performance of UKB over the Portuguese MultiWordNet with the results obtained by Agirre et al. (2014), who most recently reported on the performance of UKB as F1 over four different datasets – the Senseval-2 (Palmer et al., 2001), Senseval-3 (Snyder and Palmer, 2004), Semeval-2007 fine-grained (Palmer et al., 2001; Snyder and Palmer, 2004; Pradhan et al., 2007) and Semeval-2007 coarse-graned (Navigli et al., 2007) English all-words tasks. Although the results they present cover various disambiguation options within UKB, we focus here on the results they obtained using the *ppr_w2w* UKB method (as we have). We also assume that they continue using version 3.0 of the English WordNet (complete with information on the semantic relationships between glosses) as their underlying LKB, as they have reported in previous evaluations (Agirre and Soroa, 2009). This combination of UKB option and underlying LKB is comparable with our own evaluation of UKB over the Portuguese MultiWordNet.

The 19,700 verified synsets from the Portuguese MultiWordNet version used in our evaluation are constructed from 16,728 words, of which only 45 are not nouns. While Agirre et al. separate their results by nouns, verbs, adjectives and adverbs and also offer an overall score (2014), to compare our results with their overall score would cast our own in a very favourable (and very unfair) light. Therefore, Table 2 only compares our results against those previously reported for nouns by Agirre et al. (2014).

5 Discussion

The results presented in the previous section highlight two important points:

- That performing WSD over a smaller, language specific LKB (such as the Portuguese MultiWordNet) is *more accurate* (tagged with the sames senses as were manually assigned by a human annotator) than translating ambiguous terms into English to perform WSD over larger LKBs (such as WordNet).

- That performing WSD over a smaller, language specific LKB (such as the Portuguese MultiWordNet) produces results with *comparable accuracy* to state-of-the-art results reported for (UKB-based) WSD over the much larger English WordNet.

Table 1 shows that the results obtained by running UKB over the dictionary and graph files created from the Portuguese MultiWordNet are far higher than those obtained by first translating the target and surrounding words in the context file into English, and then running UKB over the English WordNet. This is despite the fact that the Portuguese MultiWordNet is considerably smaller, at around 19,700 verified synsets, than the English WordNet, at a reported 117,000 synsets.

Nóbrega and Pardo themselves (2014), whose approach of translating ambiguous words to English in order to perform WSD using the English WordNet we have compared with our own language-specific results, describe some of the problems that translating terms to and from English can introduce. They observe that some very specific terms or concepts in Portuguese may not have a direct translation in English at all, while conversely there may be generic terms or concepts in Portuguese that have much more specific categories in English (Nóbrega and Pardo, 2014). While their coverage may be less due to their smaller size, language-specific LKBs limit such problems, with the terminology that *is* accounted for being specific to the language in question.

A glance at the original and translated context files used in our comparison shows that in many cases incorrect translations before the WSD has even been performed have led to the difference in results using the two approaches. For example, a line from a news article in the CINTIL corpus reads:

> "O secretário de Imprensa da Casa Branca, Mike McCurry, disse que qualquer agressão iraquiana seria 'uma questão de grave preocupação'"

An accurate translation of which would be:

> "The White House press secretary, Mike McCurry, said that any Iraqi offensive would be 'a question of serious concern'"

From this sentence, extracting the open-class words in Portuguese produces the following line for the context file (formatted as lemma#pos#wordid):

> secretário#n#w1 imprensa#n#w2 dizer#v#w3 agressão#n#w4 iraquiano#a#w5 ser#v#w6 questão#n#w7 grave#a#w8 preocupação#n#w9

Upon translating each of these words to English, we are left with the following line in our translated context file, to be passed to UKB and each term disambiguated using the dictionary and graph files from the English WordNet.

> secretary#n#w1 printing_press#n#w2 tell#v#w3 aggression#n#w4 iraqi#a#w5 being#v#w6 question#n#w7 grave#a#w8 concern#n#w9

As well as a number of words which could have been translated slightly better – 'say' would have been better than 'tell' for word three, 'offensive' better than 'aggression' for word four and 'serious' better than 'grave' for word eight – there is a more obvious problem with the translation of word two. The Portuguese word 'imprensa' has been (in this context) incorrectly translated as 'printing press', the actual mechanical device used to create printed materials. With it being highly unlikely that the White House employs a 'printing press' secretary, we can see how incorrect translations from Portuguese to English would lead to UKB being provided with problematic and potentially confusing contexts from which to disambiguate target words.

Of course, we must take into account that our translations from Portuguese to English are not likely to be as accurate as those obtained by Nóbrega and Pardo (2014). They describe using the WordReference API to extract dictionary definitions of Portuguese terms in English, but because that is no longer available we instead translate terms using the linked datasets in BabelNet, as described in section 4. Because lexical gaps in BabelNet are filled using machine translation for resource-poor languages, the resources on which our translations depend are unlikely to be as accurate from the outset as those from a verified dictionary API, and it would be interesting to explore whether alternative methods of producing our translations might give different results in our future work. However, we feel that the point demonstrated by the previous example still holds true – in trying to translate ambiguous terms from Portuguese to English in order to perform WSD over a larger underlying LKB in English, we are actually introducing more noise to the problem.

Table 2 shows that the accuracy of running UKB over the dictionary and graph files created from the Portuguese MultiWordNet is comparable with previously-reported state-of-the-art results – namely running UKB over the much larger English Wordnet to disambiguate words already *in* English. As well as the results shown in Table 1 and discussed in the preceding paragraphs, showing that translating Portuguese terms into English to make use of a much larger English LKB for disambiguation decreases accuracy, the results in Table 2 show that the smaller size of the Portuguese MultiWordNet does not have any considerable detrimental effect on the accuracy of the WSD process itself.

Besides the limited lexical coverage, there is no reason that using a smaller, language-specific LKB would produce any less accurate results for WSD. In fact, while language-specific dictionaries might be much smaller in certain languages, because the semantic relationships between concepts generally hold true across different languages, graphs representing these relationships as nodes and edges can actually be created from much fuller LKBs (as we have done using semantic relations from the English WordNet). This ensures that although not all words are covered locally, our capacity to determine the relationships between them is still strong, providing consistently accurate results. Problems arise not necessarily from difficulty in determining the semantic relationships between concepts, but because the kinds of ambiguities and translation errors described above will occur when gaps in the lexical coverage of linked data are filled using machine translation.

For LOD, the implications are that while missing data for resource-poor languages can be filled in using machine translation (Navigli and Ponzetto, 2012), verified language-specific lexical resources still provide highly accurate results for tasks like WSD regardless of their comparative size – there is nothing to be gained by translating terms into other languages (such as English) to make use of fuller, larger LKBs. The increased connectivity and integration of lexical (and encyclopedic) resources in projects like DBpedia and BabelNet open up a world of possibilities for multilingual NLP, but filling the gaps using machine translation should only be a stopgap measure. Rather than abandon them in favour of the linked data already available, local efforts to grow, extend and expand language-specific lexical resources must continue, such that they can be continually re-integrated as LOD later as fuller, accurate and verified resources – thus increasing the overall quality of linked lexical data.

6 Conclusions

We have evaluated two approaches to performing graph-based WSD in Portuguese; 1) by using the smaller, language-specific Portuguese MultiWordNet as the underlying LKB, and 2) by first translating open-class words from Portuguese to English in order to use the much larger English WordNet as the underlying LKB. Comparing the results of both approaches with the human-assigned senses in a gold-standard annotated corpus, we have demonstrated that performing graph-based WSD using a smaller, language-specific LKB provides more accurate results than the approach of using the larger LKB by way of translating terms first. Furthermore, the accuracy of the language-specific approach is comparable with state-of-the-art results reported for graph-based WSD *in* English using WordNet.

For LOD, the implications of our results are that as well as in the short term making use of linked data where the gaps between resource-rich and resource-poor languages have been filled by machine translation, local efforts to grow and extend language-specific lexical resources such as WordNets should continue, so that these can be linked back to existing data as LOD later. This way, LOD will eventually consist not only of the connected semantic relationships across languages, but also fuller and verified lexical coverage, making rich multilingual NLP applications possible based on accurate linked data.

We plan to build on our work by making further comparisons to other graph-based WSD approaches, such as the disambiguation options available in BabelNet itself performed over its own linked data as an LKB, and by experimenting with alternative techniques and APIs for translating the open-class words from the context file into English in the first instance. It would also be interesting to combine approaches, augmenting results from accurate local lexical resources with results sourced via translated terms fed to larger resources. We also plan to explore whether LOD can play an effective role in the growth and extension of local lexical resources themselves, investigating whether there is an effective way that the expansion of local WordNets can be in some part automated based on manually checked and verified translations sourced from existing multilingual LOD.

Acknowledgments

This work has been undertaken and funded as part of the EU project QTLeap (EC/FP7/610516) and the Portuguese project DP4LT (PTDC/EEI-SII/1940/2012).

References

Eneko Agirre and Philip Edmonds. 2006. *Word Sense Disambiguation: Algorithms and Applications*. Springer.

Eneko Agirre and Aitor Soroa. 2008. Using the Multilingual Central Repository for Graph-Based Word Sense Disambiguation. In *Proceedings of the Sixth International Conference on Language Resources and Evaluation (LREC'08)*, Marrakech, Morocco, may. European Language Resources Association (ELRA). http://www.lrec-conf.org/proceedings/lrec2008/.

Eneko Agirre and Aitor Soroa. 2009. Personalizing PageRank for Word Sense Disambiguation. In *Proceedings of the 12th Conference of the European*

Chapter of the Association for Computational Linguistics, EACL '09, pages 33–41, Athens, Greece. Association for Computational Linguistics.

Eneko Agirre, Oier Lopez De Lacalle, and Aitor Soroa. 2009. Knowledge-based WSD on Specific Domains: Performing Better Than Generic Supervised WSD. In *Proceedings of the 21st International Jont Conference on Artifical Intelligence*, IJCAI'09, pages 1501–1506, San Francisco, CA, USA. Morgan Kaufmann Publishers Inc.

Eneko Agirre, Oier López de Lacalle, and Aitor Soroa. 2014. Random Walks for Knowledge-based Word Sense Disambiguation. *Comput. Linguist.*, 40(1):57–84, March.

Jordi Atserias, Luís Villarejo, and German Rigau. 2004. Spanish WordNet 1.6: Porting the Spanish WordNet across Princeton Versions. In *Proceedings of the 4th International Conference on Language Resources and Evaluation*, LREC '04.

Florbela Barreto, António Branco, Eduardo Ferreira, Amália Mendes, Maria Fernanda Bacelar Nascimento, Filipe Nunes, and João Silva. 2006. Open Resources and Tools for the Shallow Processing of Portuguese: The TagShare Project. In *Proceedings of the 5th International Conference on Language Resources and Evaluation*, LREC'06, pages 1438–1443.

António Branco and João Silva. 2006. A Suite of Shallow Processing Tools for Portuguese: LX-suite. In *Proceedings of the 11th Conference of the European Chapter of the Association for Computational Linguistics: Posters and Demonstrations*, EACL '06, pages 179–182, Trento, Italy. Association for Computational Linguistics.

Sergey Brin and Lawrence Page. 1998. The Anatomy of a Large-Scale Hypertextual Web Search Engine. In *Seventh International World-Wide Web Conference (WWW 1998)*.

Director General of Translation. 2006. Nova Versão da Lista de Falsos Amigos Português-Espanhol / Español-Portugués. *A Folha: Boletim da Língua Portuguesa nas Instituições Europeias (Comissão Europeia)*, 23:19–27.

Christine Fellbaum. 1998. *WordNet: An Electronic Lexical Database*. MIT Press.

Jens Lehmann, Robert Isele, Max Jakob, Anja Jentzsch, Dimitris Kontokostas, Pablo Mendes, Sebastian Hellmann, Mohamed Morsey, Patrick van Kleef, Sören Auer, and Christian Bizer. 2012. DBpedia - A Large-scale, Multilingual Knowledge Base Extracted from Wikipedia. *Semantic Web Journal*, 6(2):167–195.

Michael Lesk. 1986. Automatic Sense Disambiguation Using Machine Readable Dictionaries: How to Tell a Pine Cone from an Ice Cream Cone. In *Proceedings of the 5th Annual International Conference on Systems Documentation*, SIGDOC '86, pages 24–26, New York, NY, USA. ACM.

Lluís Màrquez, Luis Villarejo, M. A. Martí, and Mariona Taulé. 2007. SemEval-2007 Task 09: Multilevel Semantic Annotation of Catalan and Spanish. In *Proceedings of the 4th International Workshop on Semantic Evaluations*, SemEval '07, pages 42–47, Stroudsburg, PA, USA. Association for Computational Linguistics.

Rada Mihalcea. 2005. Unsupervised Large-vocabulary Word Sense Disambiguation with Graph-based Algorithms for Sequence Data Labeling. In *Proceedings of the Conference on Human Language Technology and Empirical Methods in Natural Language Processing*, HLT '05, pages 411–418, Stroudsburg, PA, USA. Association for Computational Linguistics.

MultiWordNet. n.d. The MultiWordNet project. `http://multiwordnet.fbk.eu/english/home.php`. Accessed: 2015-01-13.

Roberto Navigli and Mirella Lapata. 2007. Graph Connectivity Measures for Unsupervised Word Sense Disambiguation. In *Proceedings of the 20th International Joint Conference on Artifical Intelligence*, IJCAI'07, pages 1683–1688, San Francisco, CA, USA. Morgan Kaufmann Publishers Inc.

Roberto Navigli and Simone Paolo Ponzetto. 2012. BabelNet: The Automatic Construction, Evaluation and Application of a Wide-Coverage Multilingual Semantic Network. *Artificial Intelligence*, 193:217–250.

Roberto Navigli and Paola Velardi. 2005. Structural Semantic Interconnections: A Knowledge-Based Approach to Word Sense Disambiguation. *IEEE Transactions on Pattern Analysis and Machine Intelligence*, 27(7):1075–1086, July.

Roberto Navigli, Kenneth C. Litkowski, and Orin Hargraves. 2007. SemEval-2007 Task 07: Coarse-grained English All-words Task. In *Proceedings of the 4th International Workshop on Semantic Evaluations*, SemEval-2007, pages 30–35, Stroudsburg, PA, USA. Association for Computational Linguistics.

Roberto Navigli, David Jurgens, and Daniele Vannella. 2013. SemEval-2013 Task 12: Multilingual Word Sense Disambiguation. In *International Workshop on Semantic Evaluation*, SemEval-2013.

Steven Neale, João Silva, and António Branco. 2015. A Flexible Interface Tool for Manual Word Sense Annotation. In *Proceedings of the 11th Joint ACL-ISO Workshop on Interoperable Semantic Annotation*, ISA-11, pages 67–71, London, UK. Association for Computational Linguistics.

Fernando Antônio Asvedo Nóbrega and Thiago Alexandre Salgueiro Pardo. 2014. General Purpose Word Sense Disambiguation Methods for Nouns in Portuguese. *Computational Processing of the Portuguese Language*, 8775:94–101.

OmegaWiki. n.d. OmegaWiki. `http://en.omegawiki.org`. Accessed: 2015-07-10.

Martha Palmer, Christiane Fellbaum, Scott Cotton, Lauren Delfs, and Hoa Trang Dang. 2001. English Tasks: All-Words and Verb Lexical Sample. In *Proceedings of SENSEVAL-2 Second International Workshop on Evaluating Word Sense Disambiguation Systems*, SensEval-2, pages 21–24, Toulouse, France, July. Association for Computational Linguistics.

Sameer S. Pradhan, Edward Loper, Dmitriy Dligach, and Martha Palmer. 2007. SemEval-2007 Task 17: English Lexical Sample, SRL and All Words. In *Proceedings of the 4th International Workshop on Semantic Evaluations*, SemEval '07, pages 87–92, Stroudsburg, PA, USA. Association for Computational Linguistics.

Judita Preiss and Mark Stevenson. 2013. Dale: A word sense disambiguation system for biomedical documents trained using automatically labeled examples. In *Proceedings of the 2013 NAACL HLT Demonstration Session*, pages 1–4. Association for Computational Linguistics.

Ravi Sinha and Rada Mihalcea. 2007. Unsupervised Graph-basedWord Sense Disambiguation Using Measures of Word Semantic Similarity. In *Proceedings of the International Conference on Semantic Computing*, ICSC '07, pages 363–369, Washington, DC, USA. IEEE Computer Society.

Benjamin Snyder and Martha Palmer. 2004. The English All-Words Task. In Rada Mihalcea and Phil Edmonds, editors, *Senseval-3: Third International Workshop on the Evaluation of Systems for the Semantic Analysis of Text*, SensEval-3, pages 41–43, Barcelona, Spain, July. Association for Computational Linguistics.

Lucia Specia, Maria das Graças V. Nunes, and Mark Stevenson. 2005. Exploiting Rules for Word Sense Disambiguation in Machine Translation. *Procesamiento del Lenguaje Natural*, 35:171–178.

Lucia Specia, Mark Stevenson, and Maria Graças V. Nunes. 2007. Learning expressive models for words sense disambiguation. In *In Proceedings of the 45th Annual Meeting of the Association for Computational Linguistics (ACL)*, pages 41–48.

Lucia Specia. 2006. A Hybrid Relational Approach for WSD: First Results. In *Proceedings of the 21st International Conference on Computational Linguistics and 44th Annual Meeting of the Association for Computational Linguistics: Student Research Workshop*, COLING ACL '06, pages 55–60, Stroudsburg, PA, USA. Association for Computational Linguistics.

Mark Stevenson, Eneko Agirre, and Aitor Soroa. 2011. Exploiting Domain Information for Word Sense Disambiguation of Medical Documents. *Journal of the American Medical Informatics Association*, 19(2):235–40.

Piek Vossen. 2004. Eurowordnet: A multilingual database of autonomous and language-specific wordnets connected via an inter-lingualindex. *International Journal of Lexicography*, 17(2):161–173.

Wikidata. n.d. Wikidata. `http://en.wikidata.org`. Accessed: 2015-07-10.

Wikipedia. n.d. Wikipedia, the free encyclopedia. `https://en.wikipedia.org`. Accessed: 2015-07-10.

Wiktionary. n.d. Wiktionary, the free dictionary. `http://en.wiktionary.org`. Accessed: 2015-07-10.

WordReference.com. n.d. WordReference API Documentation. `http://www.wordreference.com/docs/api.aspx`. Accessed: 2015-06-04.

Towards the Representation of Hashtags in Linguistic Linked Open Data Format

Thierry Declerck
Dept. of Computational Linguistics,
Saarland University, Saarbrücken,
Germany
declerck@dfki.de

Piroska Lendvai
Dept. of Computational Linguistics,
Saarland University, Saarbrücken,
Germany
piroska.r@gmail.com

Abstract

A pilot study is reported on developing the basic Linguistic Linked Open Data (LLOD) infrastructure for hashtags from social media posts. Our goal is the encoding of linguistically and semantically enriched hashtags in a formally compact way using the machine-readable *OntoLex* model. Initial hashtag processing consists of data-driven decomposition of multi-element hashtags, the linking of spelling variants, and part-of-speech analysis of the elements. Then we explain how the *OntoLex* model is used both to encode and to enrich the hashtags and their elements by linking them to existing semantic and lexical LOD resources: *DBpedia* and *Wiktionary*.

1 Introduction

Applying term clustering methods to hashtags in social media posts is an emerging research thread in language and semantic web technologies. Hashtags often denote named entities and events, as exemplified by an entry from our reference corpus that includes Twitter[1] posts ('tweets') about the Ferguson unrest[2]: *"#foxnews #FergusonShooting is in a long line of questionable acts by the police. Because some acted out does not excuse the police."*

In recent work (Declerck and Lendvai, 2015) we have applied string and pattern matching to address lexical variation in hashtags with the goal of normalizing, and subsequently contextualizing hashtagged strings. Types of contexts for a hashtag can be derived from e.g. hashtag co-occurrence and semantic relations between hahstags; representing such contexts necessitates the understanding of the linguistic and extra-linguistic environment of the social media posting that features the hashtag.

In the light of recent developments in the Linked Open Data (LOD) framework, it seems relevant to investigate the representation of language data in social media so that it can be published in the LOD cloud. Already the classical Linked Data framework included a growing set of linguistic resources: language data – i.e. human-readable information connected to data objects by e.g. RDFs annotation properties such as 'label' and 'comment' –, have been suggested to be encoded in machine-readable representation[3]. This triggered the development of the *lemon* model (McCrae et al., 2012) that allowed to optimally relate, in a machine-readable way, the content of these annotation properties with the objects they describe.

While LOD enables connecting and querying databases from different sources[4], the recently emerging Linguistic Linked Open Data (LLOD) facilitates connecting and querying also in terms of linguistic constructs. Based on the activities of the Working Group on Open Data in Linguistics[5] and of projects such as the European FP7 Support Action "LIDER"[6], the linked data cloud of linguistic resources is expanding.

Our goal in the current study is to develop and promote the modeling of linguistic and semantic phenomena related to hashtags, adopting the On-

[1] twitter.com
[2] https://en.wikipedia.org/wiki/Ferguson_unrest

[3] (Declerck and Lendvai, 2010) discussed already the possible benefits of the linguistic annotation of this type of language data.
[4] A more technical definition of Linked Data is given at http://www.w3.org/standards/semanticweb/data
[5] http://linguistics.okfn.org/
[6] http://www.lider-project.eu/.

Proceedings of the Second Workshop on Natural Language Processing and Linked Open Data, pages 16–22,
Hissar, Bulgaria, 11 September 2015.

toLex model[7]. This model, a result of the W3C Ontology-Lexicon community group[8], lies at the core of the publication of language data and linguistic information in the LLOD cloud[9]. In the next sections we briefly present the current state of OntoLex, then summarize our approach to hashtag processing, after which our LOD and LLOD linking efforts are explained in detail, finally leading us to future plans.

2 The OntoLex model

The OntoLex model has been designed using the Semantic Web formal representation languages OWL, RDFS and RDF[10]. It also makes use of the SKOS and SKOS-XL vocabularies[11]. OntoLex is based on the ISO Lexical Markup Framework (LMF)[12] and is an extension of the *lemon* model. OntoLex describes a modular approach to lexicon specification.

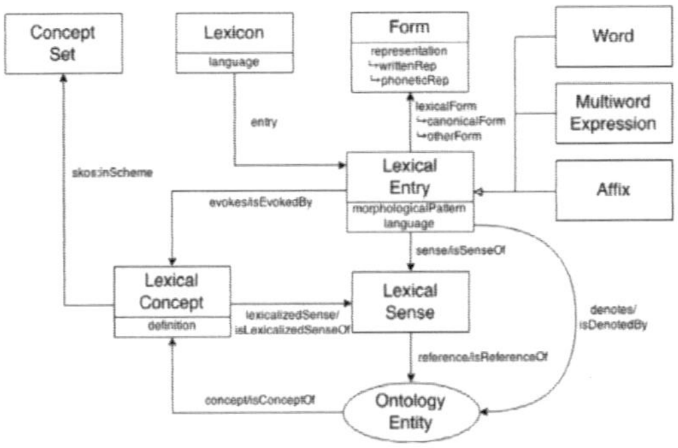

Figure 1: The core model of OntoLex. Figure created by John P. McCrae for the W3C Ontolex Community Group.

With OntoLex, all elements of a lexicon can be described independently, while they are connected by typed relation markers. The components of each lexicon entry are linked by RDF encoded relations and properties. Figure 1 depicts the overall design of the core OntoLex model.

An important relation for us will be 'reference' that represents a property that supports the linking of senses of lexicon entries to knowledge objects available in the LOD cloud so that the meaning of a lexicon entry can be referred to appropriate resources on the Semantic Web.

Additionally to the core model of OntoLex, we make use of its decomposition module[13], which is important for the representation of segmented hashtags. The relation of this module to a lexical entry in OntoLex is displayed in Figure 2.

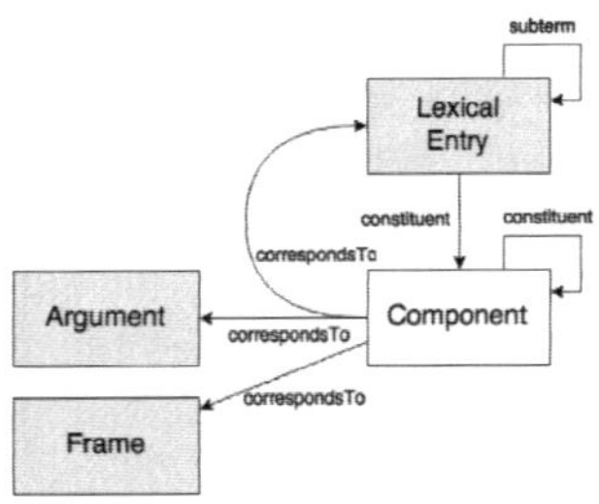

Figure 2: The relation between the decomposition module and the lexical entry of the core module. Figure created by John P. McCrae for the W3C Ontolex Community Group.

3 Hashtag analysis and decomposition

The hashtag set we work with originates from tweets collected about both the Ferguson and the Ottawa shootings[14], as part of a journalistic use case defined in the PHEME project[15]. Below we give examples of the hashtags that we encoded in a lexicon using the OntoLex guidelines:

#FergusonShooting, #fergusonshooting, #FERGUSON, #FERGUSONSHOOTING, #FergusonShootings, #OttawaShooting, #ottawashooting, #Ottawashooting, #Ottawashootings, #ottawashootings, #OttawaShootings, #Ottawa #SHOOTING, #ottwashooting, #OttwaShooting, #Ottwashooting

In Declerck and Lendvai (2015) we reported on the relation between a hashtag processing approach that we apply in our present study as well, and previous work from the literature. Our goal was to examine if hashtags can be segmented and normalized in a data-driven way. In that study, we processed a different, much larger corpus of

[7] http://www.w3.org/community/ontolex/wiki/Main_Page, and more specifically: http://www.w3.org/community/ontolex/wiki/Final_Model_Specification
[8] https://www.w3.org/community/ontolex/ and https://github.com/cimiano/ontolex
[9] http://linguistic-lod.org/llod-cloud
[10] http://www.w3.org/TR/owl-semantics/ http://www.w3.org/TR/rdf-schema/ http://www.w3.org/RDF/
[11] http://www.w3.org/2004/02/skos/
[12] Francopoulo et al. (2006) and http://www.lexicalmarkupframework.org/

[13] For details see http://www.w3.org/community/ontolex/wiki/Final_Model_Specification#Decomposition_.28decomp.29
[14] See https://en.wikipedia.org/wiki/Ferguson_unrest and https://en.wikipedia.org/wiki/2014_shootings_at_Parliament_Hill,_Ottawa
[15] http://www.pheme.eu/

tweets than the data set we take as an example in the current paper. We analyzed the distribution of hashtags and devised a simple offline procedure that generates a gazetteer of hashtag elements via collecting orthographical information: element boundaries in hashtags were assumed based on e.g. camel-cased string evidence and collocation heuristics. Using this approach on our current corpus, the hashtag *#JusticeForMikeBrown* will be segmented into four elements, while *#michaelbrown* into two elements. Subsequently, we can establish a link between *'Mike'* and *'michael'*, and type it as *lexical variant,* which we later might want to further categorize into specific types relating to normalization such as paraphrase, orthographic variant, and so on, depending on the goal.

We also proposed morpho-syntactic analysis in terms of part-of-speech and dependency analysis; the latter would detect the semantic head in a hashtag, allowing to establish lexical semantic taxonomy relations between hashtag elements such as hyper-, hypo-, syno- and antonymy. In our current study, part-of-speech information is obtained from the NLTK platform[16], while dependency information is not used.

4 Linking and exploiting LOD resources

We connected hashtags and their elements in the OntoLex model to existing linguistic and semantic LOD resources: *wiktionary.dbpedia.org* and *DBpedia*[17]. The use of other resources in the Linked Data framework, such as BabelNet[18], DBnary[19] and Freebase[20] is also relevant and will be explored in further experiments. The *lemon* model, which is the immediate predecessor of OntoLex, is utilized by wiktionary.dbpedia.org, BabelNet and DBnary.

DBpedia provides access to a rich encyclopedic resource, mainly extracted from Wikipedia infoboxes. It also provides links to popular knowledge bases such as Freebase, wikidata[21], yago[22], but does not provide linguistic information. We access DBpedia via the Python package *SPARQLWrapper*[23]. To link hashtags and hashtag elements to LOD data, we query the following properties in DBpedia[24]:

- 'rdfs:label'
- 'rdfs:comment'
- 'dct: subject'
- 'dbo:abstract'
- 'owl:sameAs'
- 'dbo:wikiPageRedirects'.

The added value of information linked via the **'dbo:wikiPageRedirects'** property is that we are able to link hashtags, or their elements, to alternative spellings and variants that were unseen in our Twitter corpus; e.g. for both hashtag variants seen in our corpus *'foxnews' and 'FoxNews',* the query returns *FOXNEWS, FOXNews, FOXNews.com, FOX NEWS, FOX News*, etc.

It is also possible to designate a preferred form of a hashtag named entity via this property, e.g. querying DBpedia for *'foxnews'* yields *http://dbpedia.org/resource/Fox_News_Channel*. Since this query returns a URL, we get an indication that it is the full span of this hashtag that designates an existing knowledge object. We use this as a heuristic for preventing our system from proposing a compositional analysis of '#FoxNews', but allow its segmentation into "Fox News". In case no such a result is returned when querying a multi-item hashtag, its segmented elements are subject to individual LOD querying and linking (e.g. *#myCanada, #besafeottawa*).

The **'owl:sameAs'** property is used to retrieve multilingual equivalents of hashtags or hashtag elements. For example, querying DBpedia for the values of the owl:sameAs property associated to *'shooting'*, returns among others the following results:

http://fr.dbpedia.org/resource/Tir
http://de.dbpedia.org/resource/Schusswaffengebrauch
http://ja.dbpedia.org/resource/射撃
http://es.dbpedia.org/resource/Tiro_(proyectil)
http://id.dbpedia.org/resource/Penembakan
http://it.dbpedia.org/resource/Tiro_(balistica)
http://ko.dbpedia.org/resource/사격
http://nl.dbpedia.org/resource/Schieten
http://pt.dbpedia.org/resource/Tiro_(balística)

[16] http://www.nltk.org/
[17] http://datahub.io/dataset/wiktionary-dbpedia-org and http://wiki.dbpedia.org/
[18] http://babelnet.org/ and (Navigli and Ponzetto, 2012).
[19] http://kaiko.getalp.org/about-dbnary/ and (Sérraset, 2014).
[20] https://www.freebase.com/
[21] https://www.wikidata.org/wiki/Wikidata:Main_Page
[22] www.mpi-inf.mpg.de/yago/

[23] https://rdflib.github.io/sparqlwrapper/
[24] The prefixes 'dbo' and 'dct' stand for http://dbpedia.org/ontology/ and http://purl.org/dc/terms/subject, respectively.

wiktionary.dbpedia.org provides an "open-source framework to extract semantic lexical resources from Wiktionary, including information about language, part of speech, senses, definitions, lexical taxonomies, and translations"[25]. For this LOD dataset there is also a SPARQL endpoint[26] that we query. A query on *'shooting'* returns a number of results, out of which we select the relevant one for our hashtag lexicon: i.e., the senses for the English noun 'shooting', given that our tweets are in English and from NLTK we know that shooting is a noun[27]:

- *http://wiktionary.dbpedia.org/resource/shooting-English-Noun-2en*
- *http://wiktionary.dbpedia.org/resource/shooting-English-Noun-1en*

Verbs and adjectives, as well as sense disambiguation is currently unaddressed in our system.

5 OntoLex Encoding of Hashtags

5.1 Lexicon

The first step in creating the OntoLex representation of hashtags is to define a lexicon that is the container for the hashtag entries.

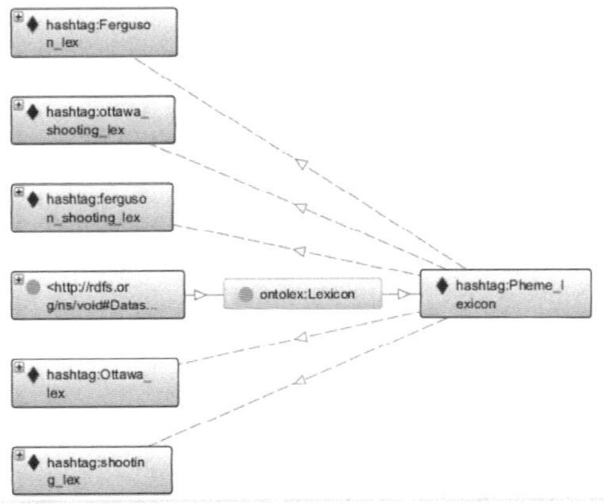

Figure 3: Graphical view of the hashtag lexicon with a entries

The graphical representation of this lexicon and its entries (here in limited numbers) is given in Figure 3[28]. Figure 4 provides the legend for arc colors displayed in all the representation graphics.

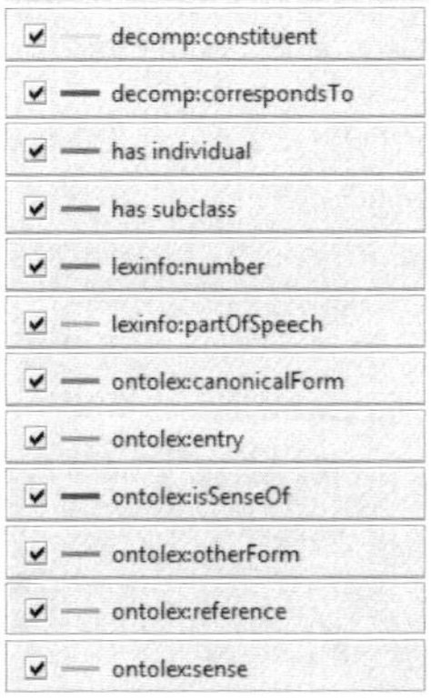

Figure 4: Legend for arc colors in graphical representations of our OntoLex model.

The RDF code underlying the representation in Figure 3 is:

```
hashtag:Pheme_lexicon
  rdf:type ontolex:Lexicon ;
  ontolex:entry hashtag:Ferguson_lex ;
  ontolex:entry hashtag:Ottawa_lex ;
  ontolex:entry
hashtag:ferguson_shooting_lex ;
  ontolex:entry hashtag:ottawa_shooting_lex
;
  ontolex:entry hashtag:shooting_lex ;
.
```

5.2 Lexical Entries

Lexical entries are instances of the class ontolex:LexicalEntry. As shown in Figure 5, the class LexicalEntry introduces three sub-classes: Word, MultiWordExpression and Affix, for now we populate the model with instances for the classes ontolex:Word and ontolex:MultiWordExpression. The corresponding coding for the entries "shooting_lex" and "ferguson_shooting_lex" is given below. We discuss the use of the property ontolex:denotes in Section 5.4.

```
hashtag:shooting_lex
  rdf:type ontolex:Word ;
  ontolex:canonicalForm
hashtag:shooting_form ;
  ontolex:denotes
<http://dbpedia.org/page/Shooting> ;
.
hashtag:ferguson_shooting_lex
  rdf:type ontolex:MultiWordExpression ;
  rdf:_1 hashtag:ferguson_component ;
  rdf:_2 hashtag:shooting_component ;
  rdfs:label "fergusonshooting"@en ;
  decomp:constituent
hashtag:ferguson_component ;
```

[25] Quotation from http://datahub.io/dataset/wiktionary-dbpedia-org
[26] http://wiktionary.dbpedia.org/sparql
[27] Details follow in Section 5.
[28] The ontology graphs presented in this paper are generated by the OntoGraf – Protégé Desktop plug-in. For more details, see http://protegewiki.stanford.edu/wiki/OntoGraf.

```
    decomp:constituent
  hashtag:shooting_component ;
    ontolex:canonicalForm
  hashtag:ferguson_shooting_form ;
    ontolex:language "en"^^xsd:string ;
    ontolex:otherForm
  hashtag:shooting_in_ferguson_form ;
    .
```

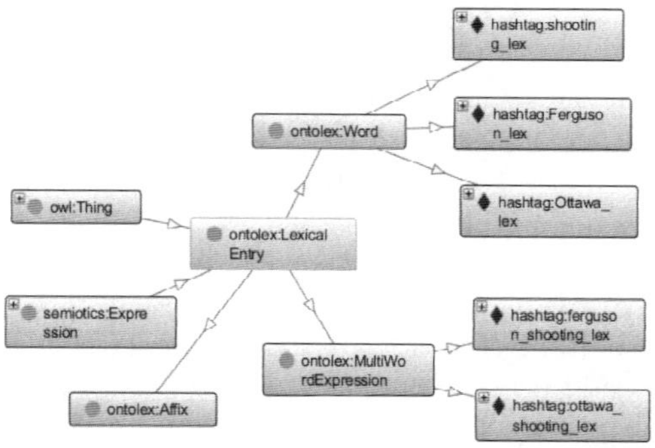

Figure 5: Subclasses of LexicalEntry, with instances for Word and MultiWordExpression.

5.3 Decomposition Module

We focus here on the "ferguson_shooting_lex" entry, an instance of the class ontolex:MultiWordExpression, to see how OntoLex supports the encoding of components of complex hashtags that have been segmented by the algorithms described in (Declerck & Lendvai, 2015). The decomposition of the hashtag is marked by the property: decomp:constituent. The value of this property is an instance of the class ontolex:Component. Since the hashtag has been decomposed in two components, the entry will introduce two decomp:constituent properties, with the current values hashtag:ferguson_component and hashtag:shooting_component

We use rdf_1 and rdf_2 as instances of the property rdfs:ContainerMembershipProperty [29] for marking the order of the two components in the compound hashtag. Keeping this information will be relevant for further contextual interpretation. The form "ferguson_shooting" is marked as preferred written representation for the entry, while an alternative form is "shooting_in_ferguson". These two forms are considered paraphrases. Other types of variants are not introduced as instances of a class, but will be added to the values of the relational data type property "writtenRep", with domain "ontolex:Form" and range string values.

[29] See http://www.w3.org/TR/rdf-schema/ for more details.

The interplay between the ontolex:Component instances and the ontolex:MultiWordExpression instances is graphically shown in Figure 6. 'Ferguson' is marked as a component, and as such it will be put to use in decomposing expressions in our corpus such as "Fergusonvigil", "FergusonPD", etc. The property `decomp:corresponds` links the components to the lexical entries in which they occur.

Part-of-speech and Named Entity information is gained from the combined use of the NLTK tagger (delivering 'NN') and the information from DBpedia that 'Ferguson' is a locality. These pieces of information are mapped to the tagset for linguistic information from the lexinfo ontology[30], which is imported into the OntoLex model.

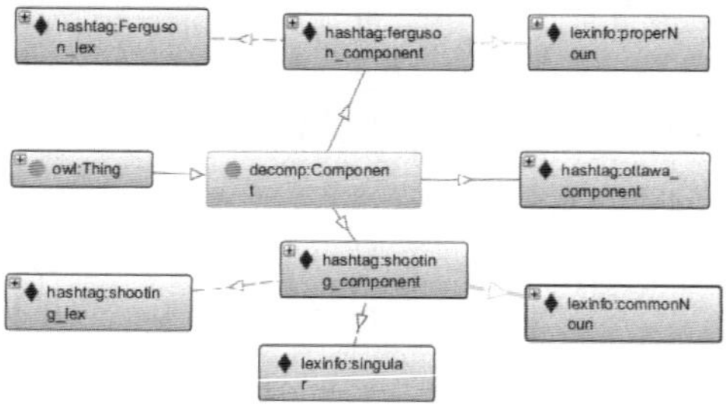

Figure 6: Interplay between components and MultWordExpression entries

Figure 7 supplies more details of the relation between instances of ontolex:Component and ontolox:MultiWordExpression, showing a component ('shooting') shared by various entries.

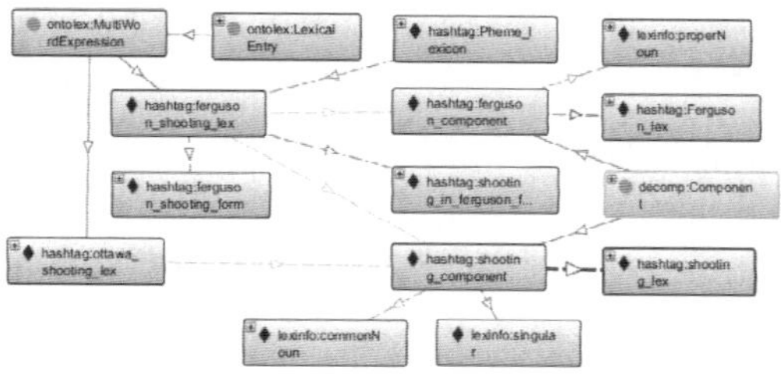

Figure 7: More details of the interplay between Components and MultiWordExpressions, showing how a component ('shooting') is shared by various lexical entries (see the yellow lines).

[30] See http://lexinfo.net/.
Figure 9 shows the lexinfo hierarchy for morpho-syntactic information.

5.4 Linking to LOD resources

In OntoLex there are two ways for linking entries to external semantic resources available in the LOD: ontolex:denotes and ontolex:reference. An example for ontolex:denotes is:

```
hashtag:Ferguson_lex
  rdf:type ontolex:Word ;
  ontolex:denotes
<http://www.dbpedia.org/page/Ferguson,_
Missouri> ;
.
```

Here we see that the lexical entry is linked directly to a DBpedia resource that contains encyclopedic knowledge, via the ontolex:denotes property. Since 'Ferguson' is a Named Entity it is important to know the type of this entity so the disambiguation task related to this string would focus on selecting the correct type. Likewise, to disambiguate common nouns, a selection of correct sense needs to be made. OntoLex offers a property to encode senses of entries, e.g. for the 'shooting' entry in the following way:

```
hashtag:shooting_lex
  rdf:type ontolex:Word ;
  ontolex:canonicalForm
hashtag:shooting_form ;
  ontolex:denotes
<http://dbpedia.org/page/Shooting> ;
  ontolex:otherForm
hashtag:shootings_form ;
  ontolex:sense
hashtag:shooting_noun_sense1 ;
  ontolex:sense
hashtag:shooting_noun_sense2 ;
.
```

The piece of code additionally exemplifies that for this lexical entry we can employ two ways to link to an external LOD resource. Either directly to DBpedia (or another source) via the ontolex:denotes property, or indirectly via the explicit listing of senses and the corresponding property ontolex:sense that has the class ontolex:LexicalEntry as domain and ontolex:LexicalSense as range. The corresponding instances of ontolex:LexicalSense for 'shooting' are:

```
hashtag:shooting_noun_sense1
  rdf:type ontolex:LexicalSense ;
  rdfs:comment "An instance of shooting
(a person) with a gun."@en ;
  ontolex:isSenseOf
hashtag:shooting_lex ;
  ontolex:reference
<http://wiktionary.dbpedia.org/page/sho
oting-English-Noun-1en> ;
```

and

```
hashtag:shooting_noun_sense2
  rdf:type ontolex:LexicalSense ;
  rdfs:comment "The sport or activity
of firing a gun."@en ;
  ontolex:isSenseOf
hashtag:shooting_lex ;
  ontolex:reference
<http://wiktionary.dbpedia.org/page/sho
oting-English-Noun-2en> ;
```

The different senses are made explicit to the human reader by the use of the rdfs:comment property. The reader can observe that via the property ontolex:reference we can also link to LOD resources, as we did earlier with the property ontolex:denotes. The main difference between the two properties is the specification of the corresponding domains and ranges, as observable in Figure 1.

Another difference lies in the fact that with ontolex:reference we link to resources encoding lexical senses[31]. This provides more precise and specific semantic information and also creates a more accurate ground for possible translations of the entries. The relation between an entry ('shooting') and its senses is graphically represented in Figure 8:

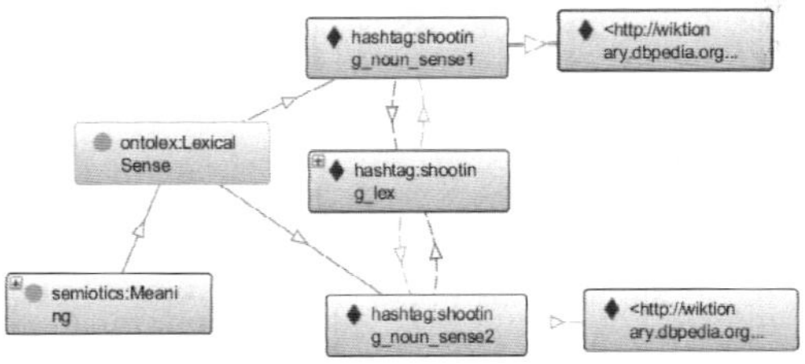

Figure 8: Relation between an entry and its senses

5.5 Part-of-Speech

Concerning the morpho-syntactic information, we map all the information obtained from the NLTK tagger onto the information structure offered by the lexinfo ontology.[32] We display in

[31] But there is no way to enforce this guideline.
[32] As a reminder: http://lexinfo.net/

Figure 9 the relevant part of the lexinfo class hierarchy. There, lexinfo:PartOfSpeech introduces 228 different categories. 'Noun' is defined in lexinfo by reference to the ISOcat http://www.isocat.org/rest/dc/1256 and http://www.isocat.org/datcat/DC-385 entries. Using OntoLex and lexinfo caters for re-using standards from the field of lexical markup.

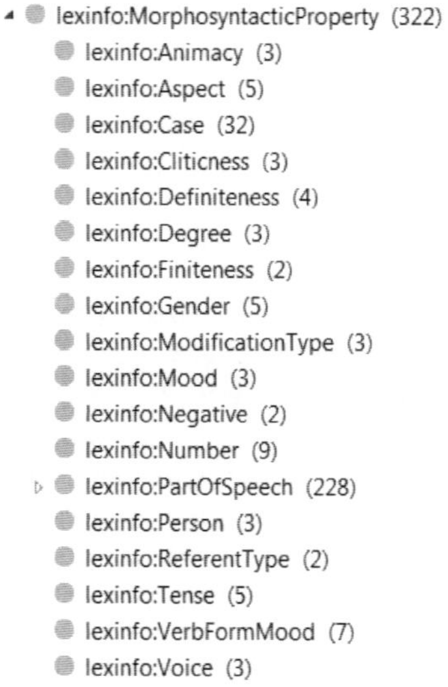

Figure 9: The lexinfo hierarchy of morpho-syntactic information.

Since we are focusing on English data which are morphologically poor, and since OntoLex does not yet provide a final model for the description of morphological information, we postpone the issue of morphological markup till an updated version of our lexical-ontology work on hashtags.

6 Conclusion and future work

We described the current status of our work on porting results of our approach to hashtags normalization onto a standardized representation format suitable for publishing hashtag data in the Linguistic Linked Open Data cloud. The OntoLex model has proven to be an adequate platform for this endeavor.

Next steps of our work will consist in applying the porting algorithm to a larger dataset. The goal is to publish the resulting data in the LLOD cloud, and so to make it semantically interoperable and machine-readable for a variety of language technology applications. To achieve this, we will also integrate our OntoLex representation of hashtags into broader semantic representations of social media data, and transfer the approach to hashtag processing and representation in languages other than English.

Acknowledgments

Work presented in this paper has been supported by the PHEME FP7 project (grant No. 611233).

References

Cimiano, P. and Unger, C. (2014). Multilingualität und Linked Data. In: T. Pellegrini, H. Sack & S. Auer (eds.) *Linked Enterprise Data. Management und Bewirtschaftung vernetzter Unternehmensdaten mit Semantic Web Technologien.* Springer, pp. 153-175.

Declerck, T, and Lendvai, P. (2010). Towards a Standardized Linguistic Annotation of the Textual Content of Labels in Knowledge Representation Systems. *Proceedings of LREC 2010.*

Declerck, T. and Lendvai, P. (2015). Processing and Normalizing Hashtags. *Proceedings of RANLP 2015.*

Ehrmann, M., Cecconi, F., Vannella, D., McCrae, J.-P., Cimiano, P. & Navigli, R. (2014). A Multilingual Semantic Network as Linked Data: *lemon*-BabelNet. In C. Chiarcos, J.-P. McCrae, P. Osenova & C. Vertan (eds.) *Proceedings of the 3rd Workshop on Linked Data in Linguistics*, pp. 71-76.

Francopoulo, G., George, M., Calzolari, N., Monachini, M., Bel, N., Pet, M. & Soria. (2006). Lexical Markup Framework (LMF). *Proceedings of the fifth international conference on Language Resources and Evaluation.*

McCrae, J.-P., Aguado-de-Cea, G., Buitelaar, P., Cimiano, P., Declerck, P., Gómez-Pérez, A., Gracia, J., Hollink, L., Montiel-Ponsoda, E., Spohr, D. & Wunner, T. (2012). Interchanging lexical resources on the Semantic Web. *Language Resources and Evaluation,* 46(4), pp. 701-719.

Navigli, R. and Ponzetto, S. (2012). BabelNet: The automatic construction, evaluation and applicationof a wide-coverage multilingual semantic network Artificial Intelligence, 193, Elsevier, 2012, pp. 217-250 .

Sérasset, G. (2014). DBnary: Wiktionary as a Lemon-Based Multilingual Lexical Resource in RDF. *Semantic Web* 05/2015; 6(4):355-361. DOI: 10.3233/SW-140147

An Ontology-based Approach to Automatic Part-of-Speech Tagging Using Heterogeneously Annotated Corpora

Maria Sukhareva[1,2] **and Christian Chiarcos**[1]
[1] Goethe University Frankfurt am Main, Germany
[2] Technical University Darmstadt, Germany
{sukharev|chiarcos}@informatik.uni-frankfurt.de

Abstract

In the LOD era, the conceptual interoperability of language resources is established by using modular architectures like the Ontologies of Linguistic Annotations (Chiarcos, 2008a, OLiA). Available as a part of the Linguistic Linked Open Data (LLOD) cloud,[1] OLiA provides ontological representations of annotation schemes for over 70 languages, as well as their linking to a reference model. We successfully train an ontology-based POS tagger on corpora with different tag sets of divergent granularity and partially compatible annotations. Making use of OLiA, we achieve interoperability of annotation schemes, and, despite sparse training data, we do not only outperform state-of-the-art POS taggers in concept coverage, but also show how traing on heterogeneously annotated data produces richer morphosyntactic annotation with no or only marginal loss of precision.

1 Introduction

Ontologies have long been recognized as a primary device for interoperability among annotations and linguistic descriptions (Farrar and Langendoen, 2003; Ide and Romary, 2004; Saulwick et al., 2005), and they have been applied to facilitate querying (Saulwick et al., 2005; Rehm et al., 2007), interoperability among modules in NLP pipelines (Buyko et al., 2008; Hellmann, 2010), or for post-processing (i.e., merging, enriching or disambiguating) the output of NLP tools (Pareja-Lora and Aguado de Cea, 2010; Chiarcos, 2010a; Hellmann et al., 2013). In this paper, we describe a novel approach towards the next challenge along this trajectory, i.e., the development of NLP tools that can directly produce and consume ontological descriptions.

In comparison with classical, string-based annotation, key advantages include a detailed assessment of classification accuracy for different annotation concepts (rather than for opaque strings representing bundles of these), a freely scalable degree of granularity (the system produces statements at all levels of granularity), and interoperability with state-of-the-art technologies from NLP and the Semantic Web. Another advantage is that annotations from different sources become interoperable, and tools can be trained on annotations from multiple corpora annotated according to different schemes.

In this regard, this paper describes a novel approach toward automatic part-of-speech (POS) annotation, and investigates the extent to which ontology-based annotations allow us to train NLP tools on corpora with divergent, but conceptually related annotations, and whether the increase in the granularity of analysis outweighs possible losses in precision arising from the heterogeneity of the training data.

2 Corpora

For reasons of interpretability, we use English corpora for this experiment, but we consider the approach to be language-independent, and (in the longer perspective) particularly relevant to less-resourced languages with a lower degree of *de facto* standardization in annotated corpora than English. Historical and modern less-resourced languages are often annotated according to a great variety of annotation schemes which can not be trivially mapped to a generalization without substantial loss of information. In order to emulate the conditions for less-resource languages, we use two heterogeneously annotated, but deliberately small corpora. Even though the amount of annotated training data is much lower than in traditional ap-

[1] http://linguistic-lod.org

Proceedings of the Second Workshop on Natural Language Processing and Linked Open Data, pages 23–32,
Hissar, Bulgaria, 11 September 2015.

	training	test	total	tag set
EWT	50,767	4,767	55,534	51
Susanne	54,109	4,886	58,995	270

Table 1: Corpus statistics: tokens , tagsets with number of POS tags

proaches, we outperform state-of-the-art taggers in concept coverage and precision (Sect. 6).

We conduct our experiments on two manually annotated corpora with different annotation schemes, namely, *Susanne* (Sampson, 1995), and the *English Web Treebank* (Silveira et al., 2014, EWB), Tab. 1.

Susanne contains annotations of 130,000 words of literary prose, drawn from the (unannotated) Brown corpus. Its hallmark is the Susanne-specific tagset (further Susa) with its high granularity and detailization of POS tags (270 unique tags). In addition, the Penn Treebank (Taylor et al., 2003, PTB) includes an independent annotation of the Susanne corpus, which enabled us to conduct the evaluation on the data annotated with both PTB and Susanne tags.

The EWT is a corpus of online reviews manually annotated with the PTB tag set. In comparison with Susanne, the lexical diversity of the EWT reviews is lower which can easily be explained by the peculiarities of the genre. Here, we use a subsection of Susanne proportional to the size of the EWT reviews and a 90:10 split into training and test corpora, respectively.

3 Ontologies of Linguistic Annotations

The **Ontologies of Linguistic Annotations** (Chiarcos, 2008a)[2] represent an architecture of OWL2/DL ontologies that formalize the mapping between annotations, a 'Reference Model' and existing terminology repositories ('External Reference Models'): OLiA solves the problem of different heterogeneous schemes by a modularized representation of annotation schemes and its declarative linking with an overarching Reference Model. Unlike a tag set, whose string-based annotations require disjoint categories at a fixed level of granularity, this ontology-based approach allows to decompose the semantics of annotations and consider all aspects independently.

The OLiA ontologies were developed as part of an infrastructure for the sustainable maintenance of linguistic resources (Schmidt et al., 2006), and within the LLOD cloud, OLiA serves as a vocabulary hub for linguistic terminology for various phenomena and resources. It currently provides ontological representations for over 70 languages with morphological, morphosyntactic, syntactic and discourse levels of annotation.

3.1 OLiA Architecture

In the OLiA architecture, four different types of ontologies are distinguished (cf. Fig. 1):

- The OLIA REFERENCE MODEL specifies the common terminology that different annotation schemes can refer to. It is derived from existing repositories of annotation terminology and extended in accordance with the annotation schemes that it was applied to.
- Multiple OLIA ANNOTATION MODELs formalize annotation schemes and tag sets. Annotation Models are based on the original documentation, so that they provide an interpretation-independent representation of the annotation scheme.
- For every Annotation Model, a LINKING MODEL defines $\sqsubseteq$ relationships between concepts in the respective Annotation Model and the Reference Model. Linking Models are interpretations of the Annotation Model in terms of the Reference Model.
- Community-maintained terminology repositories in OWL2/DL (Farrar and Langendoen, 2003; Saulwick et al., 2005, etc.), are integrated as EXTERNAL REFERENCE MODELS: Linking Models specify $\sqsubseteq$ relationships between Reference Model concepts and External Reference Model concepts.

The OLiA Reference Model specifies classes for linguistic categories (e.g., *olia:Determiner*) and grammatical features (e.g., *olia:Accusative*), as well as properties that define relations between these (e.g., *olia:hasCase*).

Conceptually, Annotation Models differ from the Reference Model in that they include not only concepts and properties, but also individuals: Individuals represent concrete tags, while classes represent abstract concepts similar to those of the Reference Model.

Figure 1 gives the ontological representation of the Susanne tag `APPGf` as an example, used for

[2] `http://purl.org/olia/`, includes PTB and Susa models

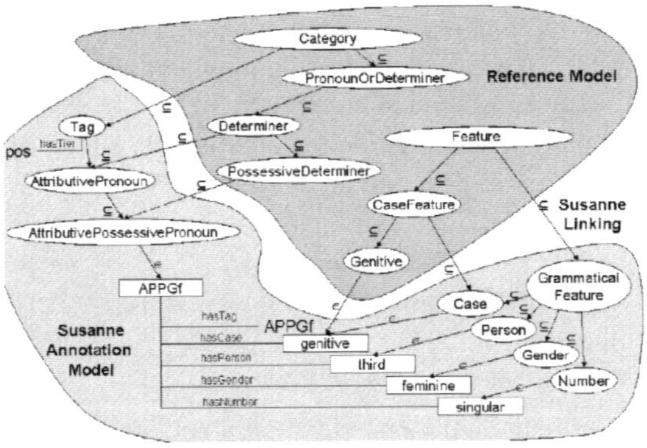

Figure 1: The Susanne tag APPGf, its representation in the Annotation Model and (partial) linking with the Reference Model, cf. Chiarcos (2008a)

her as a possessive determiner, the corresponding inheritance structure of the word class and the case property. Using the inheritance structures in the Linking Model, the tag can be rendered in terms of the Reference Model by the following OWL2 class description

$$PossessiveDeterminer \sqcap \exists hasCase.Genitive \sqcap \exists hasPerson.Third \sqcap \exists hasGender.Feminine \sqcap \exists hasNumber.Singular$$

Through ontological inheritance within the Reference Model, we can further infer that APPGf is also an instance of *Determiner* and *PronounOrDeterminer* (superconcepts of *PossessiveDeterminer*).

One important difference between this description and the (similar) description in terms of the Annotation Model is that this description is tagset neutral, and does not only apply to the English *her* as a possessive, but also to the corresponding tags in other annotation schemes (even if from different languages), e.g., the PTB tag for *her*, PRP$. Although this does provide a partial description only (*PossessiveDeterminer* ⊓ *Determiner* ⊓ *PronounOrDeterminer*), we can generalize over both tags by referring to atomic statements found in both ontological renderings (i.e., their intersection).

3.2 Related Research

Using OLiA for processing of heterogeneously annotated corpora has several benefits in comparison with other approaches. As such, we would like to emphasize that the ontology-based approach is *lossless*. Instead of simplifying heterogeneous tag sets to a common meta tag set or creating a mapping between the tag sets, we decompose tag sets into statements (triples) grounded in an ontology. This is a major difference as compared to radically reductionist approaches like Petrov et al. (2012) which inevitably lead to an extensive information loss, especially for highly detailed annotation schemes such as Susanne. A different kind of information loss frequently occurs with approaches based on a meta tag set as 'interlingua' (Leech and Wilson, 1996; Zeman, 2008): Here, a taxonomy tags is enforced from one set of languages (that the taxonomy was developed for) to another, where the pressure to stay within the pre-defined model frequently leads to 'tag abuse', see Chiarcos and Erjavec (2011) for the corresponding analysis of MULTEXT-East (Erjavec, 2004). But it also differs from more flexible, bottom-up-grown meta tag sets (Zeman, 2008), because without the implicit disjointness assumption of tags (categories) in classical tagsets, it is possible to preserve divergent, but compatible analyses, e.g., *enduring* in *capable of enduring friendships* is both a verb (morphologically) and an adjective (syntactically).

As being lossless, OLiA ensures that the information contained in the original schemes will be preserved to a maximal extent by its conceptual representation.

3.3 From OLiA to neural networks

Originally, the OLiA ontologies were conceived for conceptually interoperable information retrieval and tag set independent corpus querying (Saulwick et al., 2005; Rehm et al., 2007), but also have found a use case in NLP, so far, however, only to *represent* the output of modules in an NLP pipeline in a tool-independent fashion (Buyko et al., 2008; Hellmann, 2010), or to *merge* the output of different NLP tools in an ensemble combination architectures, where information from different sources (say, NLP tools) was integrated on the basis of the Reference Model and disambiguated using ontological axioms (Chiarcos, 2010a).

Here, we describe the first approach on directly produce ontology-based descriptions, with an ontology-based POS tagger, opening the field for future applications of ontology-based NLP which raises the current string-based state of the art of annotation in NLP to conceptual annotation processing. In order to do so, we employ a neural network architecture, as its output vector is capable to represent and to predict probability/confidence scores for all concepts and features in the ontology simultaneously, regardless of whether these are compatible with each other.

Then, for encoding and decoding annotations, *MorphosyntacticCategorys* from the OLiA Reference Model are employed. Note that for the experiments described here, we only consider these and leave morphosyntactic (and other) features for subsequent research.

4 Configuring and Training Neural Networks

We trained neural networks on EWT reviews, an equally sized subset of the Susanne corpus (Sect. 2), and on both training sets combined. The core of the algorithm is a feed-forward neural network with resilient backpropagation with the following structure:

1. 75 input neurons that correspond to three 25-dimensional word embeddings (Turian et al., 2010)[3] of the target word, its predecessor and its successor from its immediate context;
2. one hidden layer with the tanh activation function. The number of neurons in the hidden layer is heuristically set to the average length of input and output layers, thus, a natural geometric (pyramidal) design;
3. a layer of output neurons that represent OLiA *MorphosyntacticCategorys*, again with tanh normalization. The activations of these neurons represent the output vector.

The first step of our algorithm is generation of OLiA triples from heterogeneously annotated corpora using existing Susa and PTB annotation and linking models. Instead of a POS tag, every word is annotated with a set of triples, each assigning the word a *MorphosyntacticCategory* as its associated class (concept). For example, the Susanne tag `AT` for the definite article *the* is now annotated with RDF triples like *_:word$_i$ a olia:DefiniteArticle*. For the sake of simplicity, we abbreviate OLiA type assignment triples for any given word here by the assigned concept, here *DefiniteArticle*. Through subsumption inference over the ontology, every *DefiniteArticle* is also an *Article*, the full set of classes for `AT` can thus be given as {*DefiniteArticle, Article, Determiner, PronounOrDeterminer*}, for the Susanne tag `AT1` (indefinite article *a*) as {*IndefiniteArticle, Article, Determiner, PronounOrDeterminer*}, etc.

The PTB tag set is not as rich as Susa and does not distinguish between definite and indefinite articles, assigning to both *the* and *a* the tag `DT`. It conversion to OLiA thus yields the set {*Determiner, PronounOrDeterminer*}.

In the training data, the target vector is then populated with ternary values for assigned triples ($+1$), underspecified/non-predictable triples (0, i.e., not predictable from the given tag set), and non-assigned (but predictable) triples (-1) for a given gold annotation. For a tag set $X \in \{\text{PTB}, \text{Susa}\}$, T_X is the set of unique OLiA concepts predictable from any tag in X. Every cell in the output layer $\vec{y}$ thus corresponds to an assignment of a unique concept from $T = T_{ptb} \cup T_{susa}$. For a given word w_i with PTB annotation and its concept set $s \subseteq T_{ptb}$, every output node y_k with $k \in \{1..|T|\}$ is assigned as follows:

$$y_k = \begin{cases} 1, & \text{if }, t_k \in s \\ 0, & \text{if}, t_k \in T \setminus T_{ptb} \\ -1, & \text{if}, t_k \in T_{ptb} \setminus s \end{cases}$$

For, say, training on EWT, all the output values that corresponded to the concepts generated only from Susa (e.g., *DefiniteArticle* and *Article* from the example above) are thus set to 0.

Training against this data is a regression problem whose application of the neural networks to the unseen data will produce values normalized between -1 and 1 for every output node y_n, resp., its associated *MorphosyntacticCategory* concept.

5 Decoding the Output Layer

For decoding the output vectors produced by the neural network, we interpret the value of an output node y_n as a confidence score for the associated concept, with positive scores indicating high probabilities, lower scores indicating low probability (or underspecification in/lack of evidence from the training data) and negative scores indicating counter-evidence for the corresponding triple.

[3] Note that we aim to study whether neural classifiers trained over different corpora – which will show an increase in coverage (or annotation granularity) by design – will suffer in their precision. This research question is independent from the dimensionality of the embeddings, so that we chose the minimal embeddings available from `http://metaoptimize.com/projects/wordreprs`. With higher-dimensional embeddings, better results are likely to be obtained.

These scores provide a *ranking* of concepts which forms the basis to decode an output vector into a set of OLiA triples (concept assignments).

In an ideal world, the ontology provides us with consistency constraints, e.g., regarding the disjointness of two classes. At present, however, no publicly available ontology of linguistic annotation is fully axiomatized. Therefore, we employ and evaluate pruning heuristics to infer consistency axioms: *structural (path) pruning* (exploiting the hierarchical structure of the ontology), and two variants of *corpus pruning* (exploiting concept combinations observed in the training set).

5.1 Structural (Path) Pruning

In an ontology, conecpt assignments are dependent on each other: assigning class C necessarily entails assigning of its superclass C'. From all concepts with positive activation, we calculate the set P of all possible paths along the ancestor (superclass) axis in the ontology, represented as a list, e.g., $p_1 = \langle$*Determiner, PronounOrDeterminer*$\rangle$ for the PTB tag `DT`.

This set is reduced by *eliminating partial* paths: If any path p is a sublist of another path q, it is removed from P. For example, p_1 is a sublist of the path $p_2 = \langle$*DefiniteArticle, Article, Determiner, PronounOrDeterminer*$\rangle$ (for Susa `AT`) and thus to be removed if p_2 is a possible solution.

From the reduced set of non-redundant, and maximal paths P', we select the path with the highest confidence, i.e.,

$$p_{best} = \arg\max_{p \in P'} \left(\frac{\sum_{n=0}^{|p|} y_{p(n)}}{|p|} \right)$$

Here, $y_{p(n)}$ is the activation of the output neuron y_i that corresponds to the nth element in the path p. In order to prevent any bias towards longer paths, the sum of activation scores is divided by the length of the path $|p|$. Concepts that are compatible with the path but have values less than 0 (= negative evidence) are skipped.

Path-based pruning follows Chiarcos (2010b) who also assumed that classes along the subclass-superclass axis are compatible with each other, whereas siblings (and their descendants) are incompatible.

5.2 Corpus Pruning

As an alternative to structural pruning, we estimate path consistency directly out of the tags of the training corpus: Given a particular training corpus, we consider any pair of concepts compatible with each other for which co-occurrence is observed. For well-attested, frequent concepts, this is a very elegant way to enable an assignment to multiple classes. For example, an adjectival participle like *enduring* in the example above is analyzed as a verb in Susanne (`VBD`, concepts {*Ing, Participle, NonFiniteVerb, Verb*}), while in PTB, it is analyzed as an adjective (`JJ`, concepts {*Adjective*}). With a corpus having both Susa and PTB annotations, such systematic double analyses can be observed and thus, tolerated, but would be ruled out by structural Pruning.

A drawback of this method is that concepts not sufficiently attested in the training corpus may be regarded incompatible with other tags – although their occurrence would be possible, they were just too rare to be observed in the training set.

With two heterogeneously annotated corpora, we employ two variants of corpus pruning: *Disjoint corpus pruning* on each corpus individually, and *joint corpus pruning* on the merged annotations of texts in the intersection of both corpora.

With the disjoint corpus pruning strategy, concepts generated by either tagset A or B are compatible with each other if they co-occur in A- or B-annotations, any concept generated only by tagset A (or B) is compatible with every concept generated only by tagset B (resp., A).

This strategy may be too permissive, so that if A- and B-annotations for the same stretch of text are available (or can be produced using automatic tools), we merge the triple sets for every word before the corpus pruning routine applies. By doing so, we are able to learn that systematic correspondences between Susa *Participle* and PTB *Adjective* exist. This joint corpus pruning strategy, however, presupposes that a considerable body of text is annotated according to both schemes, a situation that, fortunately, we face for the intersection of PTB and Susanne (PTB$\cup$Susa referring to the Susanne corpus with both annotations merged).

6 Experimental Results

Three neural networks were trained on the training sets: EWT/PTB data only, Susanne/Susa data only, and both training sets combined. Several state-of-the-art POS taggers have been trained on this data as baseline: TreeTagger (Schmid, 1999), Lapos (Tsuruoka et al., 2011) and Stanford

(Toutanova et al., 2003), all trained and tested on the same (non-combined) data as the neural networks.

Training these on PTB annotations was straightforward. On Susa, however, TreeTagger could not accomodate 270 unique tags and was thus skipped, and Lapos could be trained but showed very low performance on the full tagset. The Stanford tagger was successfully trained using state-of-the-art MaxEnt (left3words) models for EWT and Susanne, respectively.

Like the training data for the neural network, the output of each tagger was mapped to OLiA Reference Model concepts by means of the corresponding Annotation and Linking Models. This is the basis for comparative evaluation with the neural networks.

tagset	corpus/ tool	coverage %concepts	%triples
PTB	EWT	64.9% (50)	81.2%
Susa	Susanne	85.7% (66)	85.7%
PTB∪Susa	NN:Combined	100% (77)	100%

Table 2: Evaluation: Coverage/granularity
%concepts: number of predictable concepts per tagset, relative to the number of concepts predictable from PTB∪Susa
%triples: number of NN:Combined-predicted triples interpretable against the gold tagset

Table 2 shows how NN:Combined yields a gain of informativity in comparison to the original annotations (and tools trained on that basis). Neither of both original tagsets is a proper subset of (the ontological representation of) the other one (%concepts), and accordingly, NN:Combined (with structural pruning) predicts *more triples* than can actually be evaluated against the gold annotation (1-%triples). We refer to this evaluation metric as *(OLiA) concept coverage*.

While NN:Combined trivially a gain in concept coverage over tag-based tools by design, this is logically independent from accuracy, and it may be suspected that training over heterogeneous annotations adds additional noise. Yet, as we eventually observed, it reaches the precision of state-of-the-art string-based POS taggers.

In order to evaluate this aspect, we employ two precision metrics. *Concept precision* is calculated in the conventional way with the following definitions: A predicted concept is a true positive if also generated from the gold annotation, e.g., *Noun* from both predicted tag `NNP` and observed tag `NN`. Otherwise, it is a false positive, e.g., *ProperNoun* from predicted `NNP` but not from observed `NN` (common noun).

For *path precision*, a path is considered to be a true positive only if *all* the concepts in the path are also generated from the gold tag. In the example above, the predicted tag `NNP` yields the path ⟨*ProperNoun, Noun*⟩, while the gold tag `NN` yields ⟨*CommonNoun, Noun*⟩, hence, a false positive. For conventional taggers, path precision corresponds to standard tag precision.

As shown in Tab. 2, Susa generates 66 unique concepts while 50 concepts are generated by PTB, the union of both is 77 unique concepts. To calculate concept and path precision for tag set-specific taggers (Tab. 3), concepts not predictable by the gold data are excluded from the evaluation. Thus, 18.8% of the concepts predicted by NN:Combined for the EWT test set and 14.3% predicted for the Susanne test set are ignored in the evaluation, as they could not have been generated from the original gold annotation, but only from the 'other' tag set (Tab. 2) Yet, the precision of these 'alien' concepts can evaluated on the (test set of the) PTB/Susanne intersection with double annotations (PTB∪Susa). The gold data in the test set is the union of PTB and Susa triples for the same word.

Table 3 provides overall evaluation results for the conventional taggers as well as the different neural network configurations in terms of concept and path precision on triple-represented annotations of EWT, Susanne and the merged PTB-Susanne annotations on the PTB∪Susa test set.

In general, path precision is lower than concept precision (Tab. 3). A likely reason is that tagging errors tend to occur between related POS. For example, proper nouns are frequently erroneously tagged as common nouns, but concept precision still rewards the common superconcept. Thus, the higher the granularity of a tag set, the greater the discrepancy between path and concept precision. The neural network trained only on EWT achieves the best path precision on the EWT test set, outperforming Lapos by almost 3%. The neural network trained only on Susanne outperforms the Stanford tagger both by path and concept precision. The neural network trained on both Susanne and EWT fell slightly short of the best tagger in path and concept precision on EWT, but still outperforms the best tagger (Stanford) on the Susanne test set. Furthermore, concept precision of the combined neural network on the Susanne data is only 0.3%

lower than the precision of the neural network trained on Susanne only.

Statistics over the most frequent[4] false predictions are given in Tab. 4. The first column of Tab. 4 contains the gold concept, the second column the predicted concept, the third column is the error $e_{g,t}$ for the concept pair $\langle g, t \rangle$, counted as

$$e_{g,t} = \frac{\text{freq}(concept_g, concept_t)}{\text{freq}(concept_g)}$$

The fourth column of Tab. 4 shows the contribution of $e_{g,t}$ to the total error.

For NN:Combined, the key result is that we achieve a substantial increase in coverage (18.8%, resp. 14.3%, Tab. 2) while facing only a marginal drop of precision (around 1%, Tab. 3) between individually trained neural networks and NN:Combined. The precision neural network predictions against individual corpora remains constantly high, and also for the merged test set. Furthermore, neural networks in any configuration reach state-of-the-art tagger performance; neural networks with structural pruning even outperform it, for both path and concept precision.

Tab. 3 shows little – if any – decay of precision if the neural network is trained over heterogeneous annotations of different corpora: In comparison to the best-performing conventional tagger considered (Lapos), NN:Combined (with structural pruning) loses 0.2% in path precision and 0.6% in concept precision, but yields a gain of 18.8%, resp. 14.3% in coverage.

To our surprise we found that structural pruning – which we initially regarded as being too restrictive – outperforms other decoding strategies, whereas joint corpus pruning showed the lowest precision. One reason is probably that not all deviations in annotation were eventually compatible, but that some of those mismatches were actual tagging errors, thus propagated into the neural learning algorithm. Such original annotation errors in the linguistic analyses are possibly the main reason why the performance of the combined network is slightly lower than the performance of networks trained on homogeneous data. The disjoint corpus pruning suffered less from annotation inconsistency, but its poor performance can probably be attributed to sparsity issues, i.e., rarely attested concept were incorrectly regarded as inconsistent with possible other concepts.

[4] concept frequency >1000, excluding punctuation

$concept_g$	$concept_t$	$e_{g,t}$	total(e)
ProperNoun	*CommonNoun*	30.2%	1.8%
ProperNoun	*Adjective*	16.3%	1%
AuxiliaryVerb	*Indicative(Full)Verb*	8.2%	2.5%
AuxiliaryVerb	*Finite(Full)Verb*	8.2%	2.5%
Participle	*Adjective*	5.8%	3.6%
PersReflPronoun	*DemonstrativeDeterminer*	5.8%	5.6%
PersonalPronoun	*DemonstrativeDeterminer*	21.1%	5.4%

Table 4: Confusion matrix
$concept_g$ are gold standard concepts, ordered by their percentage of the total error $total(e)$. $e_{g,t}$ is a relative count for $concept_g$ erroneously predicted as $concept_t$ to the total count of $concept_g$ predictions.

It should be noted that our NN setting was deliberately minimalistic: We used minimal context information with the smallest-dimensional word embeddings available, and trivial backpropagation without employing any more advanced procedures to improve convergency properties (e.g., deep learning). Also, we did not optimize hyperparameters but followed a simple geometric (pyramidal) structure for their initial assessment. Despite the lack of any such optimization, we were nevertheless able to prove an increase in coverage while maintaining state-of-the-art precision, thereby proving the feasibility and the potential of ontology-based neural learning over multiple heterogeneously annotated corpora.

7 Discussion and Outlook

We presented an ontology-based neural network approach to POS tagging, or, more precisely, predicting morphosyntactic categories underlying part-of-speech annotation.

Unlike other approaches trying to generalize over heterogeneously annotated corpora (Sect. 3.2), our approach is informationally *lossless*. The usefulness of such approach is obvious when dealing with heterogeneous annotations with different granularity. But also comparably-designed annotation schemes can differ in their use of apparently identical categories: POS tag semantics conflate different criteria from morphology, syntax, semantics and lexicon, respectively, but at the same time enforce categories (tags) to be disjoint. As for attributive possessive pronouns, for example, these are both pronouns (semantically) and determiners (syntactically). (Other examples for English are numerals vs. determiners, participles vs. adjectives, subordinating conjunctions vs. prepositions, various functions of TO, lexical vs. syntactic definition of auxiliary verbs, etc., so this is really

	path precision			concept precision		
	EWT	Susanne	PTB∪Susa	EWT	Susanne	PTB∪Susa
baseline taggers						
TreeTagger	77.3%	-	-	85.6%	-	-
Lapos	92.0%	16.9%	-	**95.4%**	31.0%	-
Stanford	91.4%	82.5%	-	94.8%	89.4%	-
disjoint corpus pruning						
NN:EWT Only	93.4%	-	-	95.0%	-	-
NN:Susanne Only	-	88.7%	-	-	91.4%	-
NN:Combined	91.9%	87.0%	82.1%	94.7%	90.6%	89.9%
joint corpus pruning						
NN:EWT Only	92.1%	-	-	93.9%	-	-
NN:Susanne Only	-	87.5%	-	-	90.3%	-
NN:Combined	91.2%	86.2%	76.5%	94.3%	90.0%	86.7%
structural (path) pruning						
NN:EWT Only	**94.9%**	-	-	95.2%	-	-
NN:Susanne Only	-	**90.1%**	-	-	**91.8%**	-
NN:Combined	91.8%	88.7%	**86.3%**	94.8%	91.5%	**91.4%**

Table 3: Evaluation: Path and concept precision

wide-spread even for English as the "prototypical" NLP language.) Tagset designers do not have the expressive means to state if categories overlap, so an ad hoc decision has to be made, thus naturally leading to incompatibilities between tagsets both cross-lingually and monolingually.

Using an ontology, no implicit disjointness criterion applies, but instead, every tag can be decomposed into a set of triples. This has been elaborated before by Chiarcos (2008b) and Chiarcos and Erjavec (2011). In our setting, we learn concept (and feature) assignments for every possible statement independently (and simultaneously), together with a confidence score (activation of the output layer=, and then employ *pruning* strategies to extract ontologically consistent descriptions of maximum granularity and confidence. This approach does not only guarantee consistent results, but it also is way more flexible than any string-based annotation and tools trained on that basis, whereas tags – given the likely sources of deviation in the use and interpretation of near-equivalent categories mentioned above – represent more or less opaque bundles of features.

Moreover, this allows us to combine the advantages of coarse-grained tagsets (more training data, robust categories) and fine-grained tagsets (fine-grained categories and features, but less reliably trainable on limited amounts of data). More general concepts and features higher in the hierarchy occur more frequently, and like in a small tagset that can be more robustly trained against limited training data, these can be reliably learned. Using a confidence-based ranking, this means that these concepts are *first* selected during the pruning. That is, more general concepts/features guide the choice among more fine-grained concepts/features (whose reliability is likely to improve as a result).

Also, this was an experiment in preparation for research on low-resource languages: By using pretrained word embeddings as input vectors, we reduced the need for large POS-annotated corpora, and achieved state-of-the-art results even limited amounts of labeled training data. This scenario particularly beneficial for less-researched major languages such as Hausa or Farsi for which only sparse data annotated with different tagsets is available, but where it is rather unproblematic to acquire large amounts of unannotated texts (e.g. by web crawling) to compute word vector representations.

Our findings indicate the viability of ontological models for part of speech tags: Even with overly restrictive consistency constraints applied, these guarantee consistent results. Future research will focus on optimizing parameters and explore applications of this technique to less-resourced languages and cross-lingual applications: The OLiA ontologies employed here are both cross-lingual and cross-tagset, and therefore, our monolingual use case can be easily extended to multi-lingual scenarios projection, where the output of annotations originating from difference source languages is to be combined.

References

E. Buyko, C. Chiarcos, and A. Pareja-Lora. 2008. Ontology-based interface specifications for a NLP pipeline architecture. In *Proc. LREC 2008*, Marrakech, Morocco.

C. Chiarcos and T. Erjavec. 2011. OWL/DL formalization of the MULTEXT-East morphosyntactic specifications. In *Proc. 5th Linguistic Annotation Workshop, held in conjunction with ACL-HTL 2011*, pages 11–20, Portland, June.

C. Chiarcos. 2008a. An ontology of linguistic annotations. *LDV Forum*, 23(1):1–16.

Christian Chiarcos. 2008b. An ontology of linguistic annotations. *LDV Forum*, 23(1):1–16.

Christian Chiarcos. 2010a. Towards robust multi-tool tagging. An OWL/DL-based approach. In *Proc. of the 48th Annual Meeting of the Association for Computational Linguistics (ACL-2010)*, pages 659–670, Uppsala, Sweden.

Christian Chiarcos. 2010b. Towards robust multi-tool tagging. an owl/dl-based approach. In *Proceedings of the 48th Annual Meeting of the Association for Computational Linguistics*, pages 659–670. Association for Computational Linguistics.

T. Erjavec. 2004. MULTEXT-East version 3. In *Proc. LREC 2004*, pages 1535–1538, Lisboa, Portugal.

S. Farrar and D.T. Langendoen. 2003. A linguistic ontology for the semantic web. *Glot International*, 7(3):97–100.

S. Hellmann, J. Lehmann, S. Auer, and M. Brümmer. 2013. Integrating NLP using Linked Data. In *Proc. International Semantic Web Conference (ISWC-2013)*, pages 98–113, Heraklion, Crete. Springer.

S. Hellmann. 2010. The semantic gap of formalized meaning. In *Proc. 7th Extended Semantic Web Conference (ESWC 2010)*, Heraklion, Greece.

N. Ide and L. Romary. 2004. A registry of standard data categories for linguistic annotation. In *Proc. LREC 2004*, pages 135–39, Lisboa, Portugal.

Geoffrey Leech and Andrew Wilson. 1996. EAGLES guidelines: Recommendations for the morphosyntactic annotation of corpora.

A. Pareja-Lora and G. Aguado de Cea. 2010. Ontology-based interoperation of linguistic tools for an improved lemma annotation in Spanish. In *Proc. LREC 2010*, Valetta, Malta.

Slav Petrov, Dipanjan Das, and Ryan McDonald. 2012. A universal part-of-speech tagset. In *Proc. of the 8th International Conference on Language Resources and Evaluation (LREC-2012)*, pages 2089–2096, Istanbul, Turkey.

G. Rehm, R. Eckart, and C. Chiarcos. 2007. An OWL- and XQuery-based mechanism for the retrieval of linguistic patterns from XML-corpora. In *Proc. RANLP 2007*, Borovets, Bulgaria.

G. Sampson. 1995. *English for the computer: The SUSANNE corpus and analytic scheme*. Oxford University Press.

A. Saulwick, M. Windhouwer, A. Dimitriadis, and R. Goedemans. 2005. Distributed tasking in ontology mediated integration of typological databases for linguistic research. In *Proc. 17th Conf. on Advanced Information Systems Engineering (CAiSE'05)*, Porto.

H. Schmid. 1999. Improvements in part-of-speech tagging with an application to german. In Susan Armstrong, Kenneth Church, Pierre Isabelle, Sandra Manzi, Evelyne Tzoukermann, and David Yarowsky, editors, *Natural Language Processing Using Very Large Corpora*, volume 11 of *Text, Speech and Language Technology*, pages 13–25. Springer Netherlands.

T. Schmidt, C. Chiarcos, T. Lehmberg, et al. 2006. Avoiding data graveyards. In *Proc. E-MELD Workshop 2006*, Ypsilanti.

Natalia Silveira, Timothy Dozat, Marie-Catherine De Marneffe, Samuel Bowman, Miriam Connor, John Bauer, and Chris Manning. 2014. A gold standard dependency corpus for english. In Nicoletta Calzolari (Conference Chair), Khalid Choukri, Thierry Declerck, Hrafn Loftsson, Bente Maegaard, Joseph Mariani, Asuncion Moreno, Jan Odijk, and Stelios Piperidis, editors, *Proceedings of the Ninth International Conference on Language Resources and Evaluation (LREC'14)*, Reykjavik, Iceland, may. European Language Resources Association (ELRA).

Ann Taylor, Mitchell Marcus, and Beatrice Santorini. 2003. The Penn Treebank: An overview. In Anne Abeill, editor, *Treebanks*, pages 5–22. Springer, Dordrecht.

Kristina Toutanova, Dan Klein, Christopher D. Manning, and Yoram Singer. 2003. Feature-rich part-of-speech tagging with a cyclic dependency network. In *Proceedings of the 2003 Conference of the North American Chapter of the Association for Computational Linguistics on Human Language Technology - Volume 1*, NAACL '03, pages 173–180, Stroudsburg, PA, USA. Association for Computational Linguistics.

Yoshimasa Tsuruoka, Yusuke Miyao, and Jun'ichi Kazama. 2011. Learning with lookahead: Can history-based models rival globally optimized models? In *Proceedings of the Fifteenth Conference on Computational Natural Language Learning*, CoNLL '11, pages 238–246, Stroudsburg, PA, USA. Association for Computational Linguistics.

Joseph Turian, Lev-Arie Ratinov, and Yoshua Bengio. 2010. Word representations: A simple and general method for semi-supervised learning. In *Proceedings of the 48th Annual Meeting of the Association for Computational Linguistics*, pages 384–394, Uppsala, Sweden, July. Association for Computational Linguistics.

D. Zeman. 2008. Reusable Tagset Conversion Using Tagset Drivers. In *Proc. LREC 2008*, Marrakech, Morocco.

Accessing Linked Open Data via A Common Ontology*

Kiril Simov
Linguistic Modeling Department, IICT-BAS
KIvS@bultreebank.org

Atanas Kiryakov
Ontotext AD
Atanas.Kiryakov@ontotext.com

Abstract

In the paper we present the construction of the FactForge service. FactForge represents a reason-able view over several Linked Open Data (LOD) datasets including DBPedia, Freebase and Geonames. It enables users to easily identify resources in the LOD cloud by providing a general unified method for querying a group of datasets. FactForge is designed also as a use case for large-scale reasoning and data integration. We describe the datasets, ontologies, inference rules, and manipulations done over the data. The datasets are unified via a common ontology – PROTON, whose concepts are mapped to the concepts of the involved LOD datasets. Each of the mapping rules relates a PROTON class or a PROTON property to the corresponding class or property of the other ontologies. This mechanism of constructing a reason-able view over selected LOD datasets ensures that the redundant instance representations are cleaned as much as possible. The instances are grouped in equivalent classes of instances.

1 Introduction

Linked Open Data (LOD) (LOD 2014) facilitates the emergence of a web of linked data by publishing and interlinking open data on the web in RDF (Brickley and Guha 2004). The current datasets in LOD cover a wide spectrum of subject domains – biomedical, science, geographic, generic knowledge, entertainment, government (LOD Cloud 2011). As they constantly grow, we face the problem of conveniently accessing, manipulating and further developing them. It is believed that this large set of interconnected data will enable new classes of applications, making use of more sophisticated querying, knowledge discovery and reasoning.

However, LOD is characterized by heterogeneity and inconsistency of the datasets, which makes their automated use via algorithms difficult. A lot of research effort nowadays has been focused on detecting methods to cope with and preserve the diversity of LOD, which can scale and manage their increasing growth rates. These methods bring experimental results, which show that the state of the art is still far from the performance necessary for real life applications. Highly heterogeneous contexts such as LOD and the Web need mechanisms to ensure consistency based on a set of data agreed upon or commonly acceptable, shared by various datasets, and make them interconnected. In order to provide such a mechanism we use a reference layer, consisting of one or more ontologies with different degrees of generality built on top of LOD and interlinked with their schemata and instances. This is a viable and optimal solution for handling LOD heterogeneity. In the Semantic Web, the idea of having an integrated global ontology which extracts information from the local ontologies and provides a unified view through which users can query the local ontologies is unrealistic, since it is practically impossible to maintain this global ontology in a highly dynamic environment. The idea of building reference structures at the schema level has been advocated previously (Jain et al. 2010). They state that it would be valuable to have a schema describing the subject domain of the datasets in LOD. Besides the reference layer, we think that the actual datasets in LOD needs to be tuned to fit the reference layer. Such a tuning includes: unification of modelling principles for the various datasets and cleaning the instance data that do not fit the conceptualization. In the paper we present the preparation of datasets for one LOD service including these two components: a reference layer and cleaning of the involved datasets, based on the detected conceptual mismatches between the common ontology and conceptualization of each involved dataset.

LOD are valuable source of information of NLP like extraction of vobularies, names, features. In this paper we do not discuss any concrete NLP task or application, but for each of them we need a reliable LOD dataset - the topic of the paper.

* The research reported here is done within Ontotext AD

Proceedings of the Second Workshop on Natural Language Processing and Linked Open Data, pages 33–41,
Hissar, Bulgaria, 11 September 2015.

The structure of the paper is as follows: Section 2 gives the background of our idea. Section 3 focuses on the conctruction of FactForge. Section 4 concludes the paper.

2 Background

This section outlines the three components our approach is based on: (a) conceptual schema of the world (ontologies); (b) instance data; and (c) mechanisms for inferring new information from these two sources of information. First, we provide a general overview of ontologies with emphasis on upper level ontologies. Then, we characterize LOD and describe an approach to using the LOD data with reasoning.

Ontologies. Ontologies are defined as "a formal, explicit specification of a shared conceptualization" (Studer et al. 1998). They are sets of definitions in a formal language for terms describing the world. Ontologies organize knowledge domains in concepts and relations between them. They allow for inheritance of properties and characteristics, and for reasoning according to different logics. These are some of the powerful mechanisms of ontologies that offer increased knowledge coverage, consistency, and lack of redundancy or contradiction. Depending on the generality of the knowledge domains they cover, several types of ontologies are distinguished. These are upper-level ontologies, domain ontologies and application ontologies. Upper-level ontologies, or foundational ontologies, describe very general concepts that can be used across multiple domains; examples include DOLCE [1], SUMO [2], and PROTON [3]. Domain ontologies cover the conceptualization of given subject domains. They describe concepts and relationships representative for the subject domain like biology, vehicle sales, product types, etc. The most common ontology design principles include: defining the scope of the ontology, creating a balanced class hierarchy, providing methods to evaluate the concepts and properties, as well as consistency checking. The OntoClean method (Guarino, N., & Welty 2002) is a very popular ontology design method. It recommends distinguishing between type and role when defining the concepts. It uses metaproperties to check the consistency of the ontology with predefined constraints helping to discover taxonomic errors. Data driven ontologies, such as the ontology of DBpedia [4], select the concepts based on the availability of data instantiating them.

Linked Open Data. The notion of "linked data" is defined by Tim Berners-Lee (Berners-Lee 2006), as RDF graphs, published on the WWW so that one can explore them across servers by following the links in the graph in a manner similar to the way the HTML web is navigated. "Linked data" are constituted by publishing and interlinking open data sources, following the principles of:

- Using URIs as names for things;
- Using HTTP URIs, so that people can look up these names;
- Providing useful information when someone looks up a URI;
- Including links to other URIs, so that people can discover more things.

To this end, data publishers should make sure that:

- The "physical" addresses of the pieces of published data are the same as the "logical" addresses, used as RDF identifiers (URIs);
- Upon receiving an HTTP request, the server should return a set of triples describing the resource.

LOD provide sets of referenceable, semantically interlinked resources with defined meaning. The central dataset of the LOD is DBpedia. Because of the many mappings between other LOD datasets and DBpedia, the latter serves as a sort of a hub in the LOD graph ensuring a certain level of connectivity. LOD is rapidly growing. The largest number of datasets in LOD belongs to the bio-medical domain. Another big subject area in the LOD cloud is scientific literature collection; entertainment data; government data like; Language dataetc. Finally, some datasets contain general-purpose encyclopedic knowledge such as DBpedia and Freebase, and geographic knowledge such as Geonames, etc.

The use of LOD and the development of applications based on it are difficult because the different LOD datasets are rather loosely connected chunks of information, facts, and instances. They have varying levels of completeness and external linkages. They are mainly connected at the instance level, thus losing the benefits from the enrichment of the data with implicit factual knowledge, when ontologies and schema-level mappings are involved. Even the linkage between instances of

[1] http://www.loa-cnr.it/DOLCE.html

[2] http://www.ontologyportal.org/

[3] http://www.ontotext.com/proton-ontology

[4] http://dbpedia.org/About

different datasets in the LOD cloud, via the predicate `owl:sameAs` shows drawbacks due to the fact that the instances are not described in the same way in the different datasets. They are, strictly speaking, not the same. For instance, New York's population in DBpedia is given as of July 2009, and counts 8,391,881, whereas in Freebase it is 8,363,710 as of 2008. Nevertheless, the two instances of New York from DBpedia and from Freebase are linked together with `owl:sameAs`, which implies that the two resources are fully identical. Yet, the "facts" for each instance differ. Another example points to the country of Kosovo. In DBpedia, it is described as a country, whereas in Freebase, it is denoted as a region. Still these two instances are reliably linked with `owl:sameAs`. Such divergences make the use of LOD data challenging in knowledge demanding applications or for reasoning tasks. On the other hand, introducing schema-level alignment of LOD datasets would provide significant advantages in ensuring the consistency of linkages. Such linkages would enable applications that can answer queries requiring multiple and disparate information sources. The quality of the data in the LOD cloud and their linkage are not the only challenges for the applications. The RDF datasets are supplied with vocabularies, which imply inference and generation of implicit facts. This considerably increases the overall number of facts available for exploration and poses the question of managing LOD. Using linked data for data management is considered to have great potential for the transformation of the web of data into a giant global graph (Heath and Bizer 2011). Still, there are several challenges that have to be overcome to make this possible, namely:

- LOD are hard to comprehend – the fact that multiple datasets are interlinked and accessible in the same data format is not enough to deal with hundreds of data schemata, ontologies, vocabularies and data modeling patterns;
- Diversity comes at a price – often there are tens of different ways of expressing one and the same piece of information even in a single dataset, such as DBpedia;
- LOD is unreliable – many of the servers behind LOD today are slow and have down times higher than the one acceptable for most of the data management setups;
- Dealing with data distributed on the web is slow – a federated SPARQL query that uses, say, three servers within several joins can be very slow;
- No consistency is guaranteed – low commitment to the formal semantics and intended use of the ontologies and schemata.

Using reason-able views (Kiryakov et al. 2009), described below, is one solution to the problem of LOD management. Reason-able views are the experimental setting for the approach presented in this paper.

Reason-Able Views (RAV). Reasoning within LOD with standard methods of sound and complete inference with respect to First Order Predicate Calculus is practically infeasible. The closed-world assumption for sound and complete reasoning is practically inapplicable in a web context and has never been even considered for the web of data. Due to the nature of the data in LOD in its current state, inference with them in many cases is useless, as it derives many false statements. Having datasets dispersed in different locations makes reasoning with them impractical. Reason-able views are an approach to reasoning over and managing linked data. Reason-able view is an assembly of independent datasets, which can be used as a single body of knowledge with respect to reasoning and query evaluation. The key principles of constructing reason-able views can be summarized as follows:

- Group selected datasets and ontologies in a compound dataset;
- Clean up, post-process and enrich the datasets if necessary. Do this conservatively, in a clearly documented and automated manner, so that (a) the operation can easily be performed each time a new version of one of the datasets is published; and (b) the users can easily understand the intervention made;
- Load the compound dataset into a single semantic repository and perform inference with respect to tractable OWL dialects;
- Define a set of sample queries against the compound dataset. These determine the "level of service" or the "scope of consistency" contract offered by the reason-able view.

Each RAV aims at lowering the cost and the risks of using specific LOD datasets. The design objectives behind each reason-able view are to:

- Make reasoning and query evaluation feasible;
- Lower the cost of entry through interactive user interfaces and retrieval methods such as URI auto-completion and RDF search;

- Guarantee a basic level of consistency – the sample queries guarantee the consistency of the data;
- Guarantee availability – all data is the same repository;
- Easier exploration and querying of unseen data – sample queries provide re-usable extraction patterns.

RAVs are built according to certain design principles, e.g.:

- All datasets in the view represent linked data;
- Single set of reasonability criteria is imposed on all datasets;
- Each dataset is connected to at least one of the others.

RAVs are implemented in two public services, namely, FactForge and LinkedLifeData.

3 Construction of FactForge

FactForge[5] represents a reason-able view over several important Linked Open Data datasets. It enables users to easily identify resources in the LOD cloud by providing a general unified method for querying a whole group of datasets. FactForge is designed also as a use-case for large-scale reasoning and data integration. In brief, the datasets are unified via a common ontology – PROTON, whose concepts are mapped to the concepts of the involved LOD datasets. We do this by a set of rules. Each of them maps a PROTON class or a PROTON property to the corresponding class or property of the other ontologies. This mechanism of constructing a reason-able view over selected LOD datasets ensures that the redundant instance representations (classes and properties) are cleaned as much as possible. The instances are grouped in equivalent classes of instances. Finally, the instances in these datasets are linked via `owl:sameAs` statements. FactForge development can be divided into six main steps:

1. Selecting the LOD datasets
2. Checking each dataset for consistency
3. Mapping the PROTON concepts to the respective LOD datasets concepts
4. Cleaning the datasets from any discrepancies between the concepts in the different datasets and PROTON
5. Loading all datasets in a joint repository
6. Loading owl:sameAs statements and checking for consistency

[5] http://www.ontotext.com/factforge

Here, we also present solutions for resolving discrepancies when mapping concepts from the central datasets in FactForge and PROTON, as well as the way of cleaning the datasets. In some of the cases, we have to add new instances, which are introduced via inference rules. Ultimately, FactForge provides a deeper understanding of: the Linked Open Data available on the web, some peculiarities of the datasets conceptualization and the problems of integrating the different LOD datasets.

3.1 Reference Layer Mapping Rules

This section describes the methodology for creating a correspondence between two dataset conceptualizations of the real world. When constructing such a correspondence, several manipulations of the datasets facts are conducted: (1) introducing new individuals; (2) deleting some individuals; (3) modifying some individuals; (4) inserting/deleting/updating relations between individuals; (5) inserting/deleting/updating characteristics of the individuals. The idea behind LOD is that such transformations are minimal. Ideally, there should be no transformations at all. We respect this recommendation, as much as possible, when constructing FactForge, except in cases where the resulting reason-able view contradicts with the conceptualization of the PROTON ontology. Thus, in the development of FactForge, our first aim is to support a full querying of the resulting repository via PROTON. We use only `rdfs:subClassOf` or `rdfs:subPropertyOf` statements in order to ensure a complete mapping coverage of the PROTON ontology to the other schemas in FactForge. Generally, the mapping statements can be arbitrary couples but in most cases they are simply `rdfs:subClassOf` or `rdfs:subPropertyOf` statements between classes or properties explicitly defined in the PROTON ontology, and the ontology or the schema of a given dataset. For example[6]:

[6] Here are the namespace declarations used in the document:

```
@prefix ptop:
<http://www.ontotext.com/proton/protontop#> .
@prefix pext:
<http://www.ontotext.com/proton/protonext#> .
@prefix owl: <http://www.w3.org/2002/07/owl#> .
@prefix rdf: <http://www.w3.org/1999/02/22-rdf-
syntax-ns#> .
@prefix rdfs: <http://www.w3.org/2000/01/rdf-
schema#> .
@prefix dbp: <http://dbpedia.org/ontology/> .
@prefix dbp-prop:<http://dbpedia.org/property/> .
@prefix fb: <http://rdf.freebase.com/ns/> .
```

```
dbp:SportsTeam
  rdfs:subClassOf  pext:Team .
foaf:homepage
  rdfs:subPropertyOf  pext:hasWebPage .
```

However, due to the different conceptualizations, in some cases a more complex mapping is needed. For example, in the Geonames dataset geographical objects are classified by codes and not by an ontology hierarchy. In such cases the mapping is done by more complex statements such as:

```
[ rdf:type owl:Restriction ;
  owl:onProperty geo-ont:featureCode ;
  owl:hasValue geo-ont:A.PCL ]
      rdfs:subClassOf pext:Country .
```

Some of these compound statements require adding new individuals. In such cases, we use the OWLIM inference rules to create the necessary additions. Here is an example:

```
//dbp-ont:PrimeMinister rdfs:subPropertyOf
// [ptop:hasPosition [pupp:hasTitle]].
  Id:PM
      p  <rdf:type> <dbp-ont:PrimeMinister>
     -------------------------------------
      p <ptop:hasPosition> j
      j <pext:hasTitle> <pext:PrimeMinister
```

Here, the inference rule is necessary because the conceptualizations in the DBPedia ontology and in the PROTON ontology are different. In DBPedia, Prime Minister belongs to a class of politicians, which is a class of person, while in PROTON, Prime Minister is a title of a job position. Thus, in DBPedia, a given Prime Minister is an individual whereas in PROTON he is an individual who has a position PrimeMinister. Since the instance data about the position itself (j in the rule above) is missing in the DBPedia dataset, it has to be created so that the mapping between the two ontologies is consistent.

3.2 Cleaning Two LOD datasets

In this section we present two of the most popular LOD datasets - DBPedia and Freebase with respect to discrepancies between their conceptualization and ontology in the reference layer.

DBPedia Ontology and Dataset. The DBPedia dataset is created by extracting structured information from Wikipedia and presenting it in an RDF form (http://dbpedia.org/About). The conceptualization of the DBPedia dataset is based on the categories that are designed and implemented in Wikipedia, i.e. the data in the info-box section of the articles. This conceptualization is presented as an ontology. For our purposes, we have used version 3.8. It contains 359 classes, 800 object properties and 975 data types. The instances in the DBPedia dataset are classified according to the conceptual information in its ontology and some other well-known ontologies like: http://schema.org and http://xmlns.com/foaf/spec/. In addition, some of the classes and properties of these other ontologies are used in the definition of the DBPedia ontology. In the majority of cases, the conceptualizations of the DBPedia and PROTON ontologies are compatible and the mapping between them is straightforward as discussed earlier. However, there are still some differences as illustrated in the following two examples:

Architect as a Person. In the DBPedia ontology, many roles in society, mainly performed by persons, are formalized as subclasses of the class dbp-ont:Person.

```
dbp-ont:Architect
      rdf:type owl:Class;
      rdfs:subClassOf dbp-ont:Person .
```

The definition in PROTON is:

```
pext:Architect
 rdf:type pext:Profession ;
 rdfs:comment "A profession of planning,
    design and oversight of the
    construction of buildings and some
    other artefacts. (Wikipedia)"@en .
```

and

```
pext:Profession
  rdf:type owl:Class ;
  rdfs:subClassOf pext:SocialFunction .
```

The main difference is that in PROTON the class pext:Architect is defined as a profession and a social function, in order for someone (or something) to have this profession. This means that not only persons can perform it. While in DBPedia the definition follows the logic that all architects described in Wikipedia are, in fact, persons. It is relatively easy to overcome such conceptual differences by an appropriate mapping between the two ontologies:

```
dbp-ont:Architect rdfs:subClassOf
  [ rdf:type owl:Restriction ;
    owl:onProperty pext:hasProfession ;
    owl:hasValue pext:Architect ] .
```

This statement determines that all instances of `dbp-ont:Architect` correspond to the instances of the PROTON ontology with the profession `pext:Architect`.

Sport as an Activity. Another example is the definition of Sport. DBPedia defines it as follow:

```
dbp-ont:Sport
```

@prefix foaf: <http://xmlns.com/foaf/0.1/> .

```
    rdf:type owl:Class;
  rdfs:comment "A sport is commonly
    defined as an organized,
    competitive, and skillful
    physical activity."@en;
  rdfs:subClassOf dbp-ont:Activity .
```

and PROTON defines it as:

```
pext:Sport
 rdf:type owl:Class ;
 rdfs:comment "A specific type of
       sport game"@en ;
 rdfs:subClassOf pext:SocialAbstraction.
```

The difference is that in DBPedia, Sport is a specific activity and its characteristics such as game rules, number of participants, etc. are not defined in the class `dbp-ont:Sport`. In PROTON the characteristics of the sport game are defined in the class `pext:Sport` as a social abstraction. The actual realization of the definition as a sport event is an instance of activity. Unfortunately, any mapping between the two ontologies cannot solve this conceptual difference. The following mappings:

```
dbp-ont:Activity
  rdfs:subClassOf pext:Activity .
```

and

```
dbp-ont:Sport
  rdfs:subClassOf pext:Sport .
```

automatically make all instances of the class `dbp-ont:Sport` in PROTON to be simultaneously instances of the classes `ptop:Happening` and `ptop:Abstract`, which are mutually disjoint.

In FactForge such conceptualization differences between the two ontologies are solved by not loading the DBPedia ontology into the FactForge repository. In this way, we make use of the richness of the DBPedia instances but impose the conceptualization of PROTON ontology over it.

Another reason for not loading the DBPedia ontology is that the definitions in the DBPedia ontology also contain mappings to other ontologies. However, we believe that including ontology statements referring to classes (properties, etc) of other ontologies is not a good practice. First, presenting the necessary conceptualization requires importing the other ontology. And second, this can introduce some contradictions in the ontology that uses these statements. For example, the DBPedia ontology contains some statements from the Schema ontology (http://schema.org). However, because DBPedia is not an extension of the Schema ontology, therefore it is better to store these statements separately. If they are included in the definitions of the DBPedia classes, this can lead to some contradictions as illustrated in the examples below for University and College:

```
dbp-ont:University
 rdf:type owl:Class;
 rdfs:subClassOf
      dbp-ont:EducationalInstitution ;
 owl:equivalentClass
      schema:CollegeOrUniversity .
```

and

```
dbp-ont:College a owl:Class;
 rdf:type owl:Class;
 rdfs:subClassOf
     dbp-ont:EducationalInstitution ;
 owl:equivalentClass
     schema:CollegeOrUniversity .
```

Using `owl:equivalentClass` makes these two classes - `dbp-ont:University` and `dbp-ont:College` - the same. Such equivalent statements are difficult to be noticed in the DBPedia ontology as it is full of them but it is also not very easy to use DBPedia without such statements. The instance data also contains statements that result from inferences from the DBPedia ontology. In order to avoid all conceptualizations that follow from the DBPedia ontology we have to clean the DBPedia instance data from such inferences. Here are some examples:

Subclass - Superclass inference. In the DBPedia instance data, each instance of sport is classified as sport but also as an activity. Therefore, even if we do not load the DBPedia ontology into the FactForge repository, this inference is present in the instance data. Thus, the classification of the DBPedia sport instances will also be wrong in PROTON when mapping PROTON to DBPedia. To clean this instance data statement we have created a deletion statement of the following type:

```
delete {?s a dbp-ont:SuperClass} where
    { ?s a dbp-ont:SubClass .
      ?s a dbp-ont:SuperCLass . }
```

Here is an example:

```
delete {?s a dbp-ont:Activity} where
    { ?s a dbp-ont:Sport .
      ?s a dbp-ont:Activity . }
```

In this way, if there is a statement for a subclass, we delete all the statements for the super classes. After that, we use the inference mechanisms of the repository to make the inferences that follow from the mapping to the PROTON ontology.

rdfs:domain and rdfs:range statements. In the DBPedia instance data, some statements for domain and range have properties connected to instances that do not belong to the appropriate classes. Such unclassified instances in DBPedia could be wrongly classified in PROTON, based on these domain and range statements. In order to clean such cases we use queries of the following type:

```
delete {?s dbp-ont:dbpediaProperty ?y }
where
{?s dbp-ont:dbpediaProperty ?y .
 ?y rdf:type ?c .
filter(
         ?c = dbp-ont:Class01
     ||   ?c = dbp-ont:Class02
     ||   ...
     ## List of all unappropriate classes
     )
}
```

Here is part of an example of the property `dbp-ont:birthPlace`.

```
delete {?s dbp-ont:birthPlace ?y } where
{?s dbp-ont:birthPlace ?y .
 ?y rdf:type ?c .
filter(?c = dbp-ont:AcademicJournal
   ||   ?c = dbp-ont:Activity
   ||   ?c = dbp-ont:AdministrativeRegion
...
        )
}
```

Apart from the deleted statements discussed earlier, we have deleted all instance data described by statements using classes that are not from the DBPedia ontology. In this way, the DBPedia instance data has a clean interpretation in terms of the PROTON conceptualization.

Freebase Dataset. Freebase7 is a community-curated database of well-known people, places, and things. In Freebase, real-world entities are represented as topics. There are topics for movie stars, countries, cities, etc. The information for each topic is structured in three levels as defined in the Freebase schema. The first layer comprises several domains (76). Each domain is defined by type (second layer) and each type has properties (third layer). The types are connected via the special relation inclusion of type. This relation connects more specific types with more general types: the type fb:base/litcentral/named_person includes the type: fb:people/person. It is not possible to interpret this relation as superclass-to-subclass relation, because it is not strict in the sense that each instance of the subclass inherits the properties of the instance of the super class. For example, the type fb:film/actor also includes the type fb:people/person. But its definition is: "The Film Actor type includes people (and credited animals) who have appeared in any film ...". Therefore, in most cases, the instances of the type fb:film/actor are people but there are also cases where they are not. Thus, the interpretation of the type inclusion relation is not strict with respect to inheritance of the properties from the included type. In the example above, if the film actor is a person, then he or she inherits all properties from the type for persons. But if it is not a person, then it does not inherit any of these properties. Instead, it inherits properties from some other type(s).

These peculiarities of the Freebase schema impose some restrictions over the mapping to the PROTON ontology. Mapping so many types and properties requires more extensive work. Therefore, for our purposes, we have mapped only the types with more than 500 instances in the Freebase dataset to the PROTON concepts. Another criterion is that the mapping does not produce any misclassification of some instances. For many types the mapping is straightforward:

```
fb:location.location
  rdf:type owl:Class;
  rdfs:comment "The Location type is
   used for any topic with a fixed
   location..."@en ;
  rdfs:label "Location";
       rdfs:subClassOf ptop:Location .
```

For types representing professions and other social roles, the mappings are similar to the mapping used for the DBPedia ontology:

```
  fb:military-militarycommander
    rdfs:subClassOf
      [rdf:type owl:Restriction ;
       owl:onProperty pext:hasTitle ;
       owl:allValuesFrom
pext:Commander].
```

Some of the types are mediators between a type and a grouping of several other types. This is mainly used to represents event information. For example, the type *Website ownership* describes an event of owning a website by an agent for some period. A website can be owned by different agents in different periods, thus it is important that these 'owning' events are represented as different instances in the dataset.

At present, we have not yet mapped the mediator types to PROTON. For this type of mapping it is necessary to use an appropriate subclass of the class ptop:Happening. For example, the type *Website ownership* can be mapped to a subclass of the class ptop:Situation, where the start and end date of the ownership are stated, the owner and the address of the website are specified, etc. As this requires huge extension of PROTON, it is not featured in the current version.

[7] http://www.freebase.com/

In the original dataset, there are also several errors in the instance classification. For example, organisation and location are very often represented by the same instance. More specifically, the types `fb:organization.organization` and `fb:location.location` have 42763 instances in common. We believe that such cases result from the linguistic intuition of the users who created the data in question. In many cases, the same word denotes both the meaning of an institution and a location. We do not consider this a good practice for the semantic representation in LOD and we think that it should be avoided. The different classes (types in Freebase) have different properties. Although the Freebase types are not strict in inheriting properties, some types are still not mutually compatible (intuitively). For example, due to this misclassification, the instance of the United States of America (https://www.freebase.com/m/09c7w0) is not only an instance of the types Country, Location but also of Food. We believe that such knowledge has to be represented in a different way.

It is important to note that correcting such cases of instances classification to many disjoint types (classes) is outside the scope of the current version of FactForge. In future, we envisage to introduce new instances for each disjoint class and to keep relations between them where necessary via appropriate properties. Although we could perform such an extension of Freebase, in our view, it is better this to be done in the original dataset. We consider these mismatches as a result from crowdsourcing where some of the providers of knowledge where influenced by the semantics of natural language.

4 Conclusion

In this paper we present some problems in accessing LOD via a common ontology. The main problems of using this approach with respect to involved datasets are demonstrated via examples from two of the most popular LOD datasets: DBPedia and Freebase. The main lessons learned are as follows:

1. The world can be modelled in many different ways, which can be formally incompatible but still understandable by human users. It is true that the main value of a dataset is in its usefulness to the stakeholders. However, this is not enough in terms of the Semantic Web where the goal is to have LOD datasets that can be processed by machines. To achieve this, it is necessary to apply some formal evaluation of the represented knowledge.
2. The incompatibility can appear on different levels: granularity of conceptualization, representation of different kinds of knowledge (for example, the difference between sortals and roles), etc. Generally, the conclusion is that if we want LOD to achieve their goals, they should not only follow some formats but also their conceptualizations should adhere to certain restrictions and ensure compatibility.
3. Constructing new ontologies based on existing ones has to incorporate the complete semantics of the corresponding ontologies instead of just fragments of them. Such an approach will have an effect on the consistency of the new ontologies and their interoperability with the existing ones.

In our view LOD needs more requirements on semantic level in order to be more reliable web of semantically linked open data..

Acknowledgements

This work was partially supported by MULTISENSOR project (FP7-610411) .

References

Linking Open Data. Retrieved from W3C Semantic Web Education and outreach community project: http://linkeddata.org/. (2014).

Brickley D., & Guha R.V. RDF Vocabulary Description Language 1.0: RDF Schema. W3C Recommendation 10 February 2004. http://www.w3.org/TR/rdf-schema/. (2004).

State of the LOD Cloud. Retrieved from http://www4.wiwiss.fu-berlin.de/lodcloud/state. (2011).

Jain, P., Hitzler, P., Sheth, A. P., Verma, K., & Yeh, P. Z. Ontology Alignment for Linked Open Data. In Patel-Schneider, Y. P. P. (Ed.), Proceedings of the 9th International Semantic Web Conference. Shanghai. (2010).

Studer R, Benjamin V. R., & Fensel D. Knowledge Engineering: Principles and Methods. IEEE Transactions on Data and Knowledge Engineering , 25 ((1-2)), pp. 161-199. (1998).

Guarino, N., & Welty, C. Evaluating Ontological Decisions with OntoClean. Communications of the ACM, 45(2) , pp. 61-65. (2002).

Berners-Lee, T. Design Issues: Linked Data. Retrieved from http://www.w3.org/DesignIssues/LinkedData.html. (2006).

Heath, T., & Bizer, C. Linked Data: Evolving the Web into a Global Data Space. (J. H. (eds.), Ed.) Synthesis Lectures on the Semantic Web: Theory and Technology (1:1), 1-136. (2011).

Kiryakov, A., Ognyanoff, D., Velkov, R., Tashev, Z., & Peikov, I. LDSR: Materialized Reason-able View to the Web of Linked Data. In R. H. Patel-Schneider (Ed.), Proceedings of OWLED 2009 . Chantilly, USA. (2009).

The GuanXi network: a new multilingual LLOD for Language Learning applications

Ismail El Maarouf[1], Eugene Alferov[2], Doug Cooper[3], Zhijia Fang[4], Hatem Mousselly-Sergieh[5], Haofen Wang[6]
[1]University of Wolverhampton, United Kingdom. [2]Kherson State University, Ukraine.
[3]CRCL, USA. [4,6]East China University of Science and Technology, China.
[5]Ubiquitous Knowledge Processing Lab, Technische Universität Darmstadt, Germany.
[1]i.el-maarouf@wlv.ac.uk, [2]alferov.evgeniy@gmail.com,
[3]doug.cooper.thailand@gmail.com, [4]fantorm030@gmail.com,
[5]mousselly-sergieh@ukp.informatik.tu-darmstadt.de,
[6]whfcarter@ecust.edu.cn

Abstract

Linguistic resources are essential for Language Learning applications. However, available resources are usually created in isolation, thus, they are scattered and need to be linked before they can be used for a specific task such as learning of a foreign language. To address these problems we present a new resource that link linguistic resources of multiple languages using the framework of Linguistic Linked Open Data (LLOD).

1 Introduction

This paper presents the GuanXi[1] network, a multilingual Linguistic Linked Open Data (LLOD) resource. GuanXi is to be integrated in a language learning platform to provide course designers with easy access to quality language data on a variety of media (text, audio, video, image) in order to support the construction of learning activities, but also harvest the power of Linked Data to suggest new views on data, as well as new activities.

For this particularly sensitive application, the GuanXi network provides reliable linked data where links are of high quality. GuanXi currently focuses on verbs and draws on recent RDF conversions of various LLOD such as PDEV-lemon (El Maarouf et al., 2014), Slovnyk and COW (Wang and Bond, 2013).

This paper presents this network and the methods used to build it and evaluate the multilingual sense links. The work presented here focuses on techniques where WordNet[2] is used as an interlingual index, and where corpus data can be leveraged, integrated, and connected to the lexical entries at the level of sense. Corpus data is particularly important for language learning as it provides massive amounts of real language use.

Section 2 describes related work on resources and technologies of sense linking. Section 3 presents the resources integrated in the GuanXi Network. Section 4 presents the different methods used to build the GuanXi network for each language pair, depending on available resources and section 5 presents the data model using the LLOD framework. Section 6 provides both automatic and manual evaluations of sense linking strategies and section 7 concludes on future work.

2 Related Work: sense linking

A major concern of Linked Data (LD) is to meaningfully interconnect resources in a way that is consistent and reliable. For Linguistic LD (LLD), this implies that introducing links at the level of the sense is of a much higher quality and usefulness than at the level of, say, the entry. This is because each lexical entry may offer a number of senses and, since words can be polysemous, getting the sense wrong will lead to disastrous consequences or limited progress, for any application that makes use of the resource. It is important to note that this is not specifically an issue of LLD, but of language processing in general and semantics. Overall, linking entities belonging to two different resources consist in automatically extracting existing information relevant to each entity within each resource and compute a similarity for each possible link.

Methods include aligning senses of different resources (e.g. WordNet and FrameNet) based on the similarity of the corresponding glosses/definitions. This technique was used in UBY (Gurevych et al., 2012; Niemann and Gurevych, 2011) where the alignment between

[1]Literaly, guanxi, or 关系, is Chinese for relationship.
[2]http://wordnet.princeton.edu/

Proceedings of the Second Workshop on Natural Language Processing and Linked Open Data, pages 42–51,
Hissar, Bulgaria, 11 September 2015.

two senses is determined based on the cosine similarity of their gloss representations. Another family of approaches for word-sense alignment uses graph methods, such as personalized page rank (PPR) (Agirre and Soroa, 2009), Dijkstra-WSA (Matuschek and Gurevych, 2013) and BabelNet (Navigli and Ponzetto, 2012).

Techniques for aligning senses from resources of different languages have also been proposed, mainly by applying Machine Translation to get translated glosses, and compute in a second step the similarity. This is, for instance, the method used in UBY to connect OmegaWiki and WordNet (Gurevych et al., 2012; Bond and Foster, 2013). Because these methods rely on definitions, they are very similar to Lesk similarity variants in Word Sense Disambiguation (WSD) (Lesk, 1986; Banerjee and Pedersen, 2002), which compute the similarity between a definition and an example in order to assign the correct sense.

Following that, methods making use of corpus data have been proposed. BabelNet is the result of (among other things) harvesting sense-tagged corpora and their automatic translation by Google Translate of WordNet annotated SemCor and Wikipedia (Navigli and Ponzetto, 2012). Babelnet also makes use of graph-based methods (Mihalcea, 2005; Navigli and Ponzetto, 2012).

BabelNet contains lexical data for over 270 languages and can be accessed through a WSD service, named Babelfy, which automatically annotates the sense of each content word in a sentence from any of the 270 languages. Babelfy uses a unified graph-based approach that combines Event Linking (EL) and WSD techniques. Given a text that should be disambiguated, all linkable fragments are extracted and for each fragment, a list of a candidate senses is extracted according to a semantic network. The semantic network contains a signature for each concept, that is, a set of related concepts. Next,a graph-based semantic interpretation for the input text is created, by linking the candidate senses of the extracted fragments using the previously-computed semantic signatures. Finally, a dense subgraph of this representation is extracted and the best candidate sense for each fragment is selected.

However, the techniques described in this section have unsatisfying accuracy, as much of the information is missing, and (automatic) Word Sense Disambiguation is still not solved (Kilgarriff and Palmer, 2000; Navigli, 2009), and is generally around 70% accuracy. The best way to link linguistic data accurately therefore still depends ultimately on lexicographical expertise. This is, for instance, the approach taken in WordNets (Bond and Paik, 2012).

Using lexicographic expertise to identify sense links should avoid (resource) publication bias, experiments and resources bootstrapping on the same data over and over again, and will open new perspectives. Note that using lexicographic expertise does not mean that automatic methods should be discarded; in fact the approach described in this paper makes use of semi-automatic methods for dataset linking, and lexicographer input is kept to the evaluation stage of the cycle. This paper explores the idea that the main concern for accurate LLD is to design efficient frameworks to make the best use of Human expertise in a minimum of time.

3 Target Resources

In aligning lexical resources, WordNet is almost inescapable as the English WordNet is manually connected to several languages (but see (Sérasset, 2012), for a different approach). However, comparatively few resources/languages are connected to WordNet. Even BabelNet has limited coverage for languages which are less resourced than English (e.g. Ukrainian). Moreover, other lexical resources exist even for English that contain valuable knowledge but are not connected. This section provides a short description of the resources used in this paper.

3.1 The Pattern Dictionary of English Verbs (PDEV)

PDEV [3] is a dictionary of English verbs. It is based on a new technique, called Corpus Pattern Analysis (CPA)(Hanks and Pustejovsky, 2005; Hanks, 2012; Hanks, 2013; Baisa et al., 2015), for mapping meaning onto words in text. CPA is also influenced by frame semantics (Fillmore, 1985) and PDEV can be seen as complementary to FrameNet[4]. Where FrameNet offers an in-depth analysis of semantic frames, CPA offers a systematic analysis of the patterns of meaning and use of each verb. Each CPA pattern can in principle be plugged into a FN semantic frame. In PDEV verb patterns consist not only of the basic "argument

[3] http://pdev.org.uk

[4] https://framenet.icsi.berkeley.edu/

structure" or "valency structure" of each verb, but also of subvalency features, where relevant, such as the presence or absence of a determiner in noun phrases constituting a direct object. Each argument in a PDEV pattern is populated with Semantic Types (taken from a shallow semantic ontology[5]) indicating the preferred semantic set of entities which are prototypically found in each slot. PDEV is a unique resource in this regard. It is also the output of a corpus-based lexicographical approach and provides extensive sets of examples from real language data.

PDEV has recently been converted into RDF (El Maarouf et al., 2014) using the lemon model (McCrae et al., 2011). PDEV-lemon contains 17,634 triples, 3,702 patterns/senses for 984 entries and the dump obtained for this paper covers an up-to-date lexicon of 1,273 entries and 4,531 patterns/senses.

3.2 Chinese Open Wordnet (COW)

The Chinese Open Wordnet (COW) is a large scale, free dictionary for Mandarin Chinese (Wang and Bond, 2013). COW was created to address the main limitations of other Chinese WordNets, namely the coverage and the quality of the data. To achieve this, a three-phase procedure was applied:

1. data was extracted from the Wikitionary[6] and merged with SEW (Southwest University WordNet) (Xu et al., 2008),
2. manual check was performed on the translations, and
3. the semantic relations were also checked manually.

Currently, COW includes 42,315 synsets with 79,812 senses and 61,536 unique words.

3.3 Slovnyk Dictionary

Slovnyk[7] is a multilingual dictionary that supports bilingual translation among 32 languages. For a word in a source language, Slovnyk provides the corresponding translation in the target language according to the most common sense of the source word. In contrast to WordNet, Slovnyk does not provide grammatical information, sense information, or semantic relation between terms. In this paper, we obtained a subset of Slovnyk for two language pairs: English - Ukrainian, and Ukrainian - Spanish. This has been converted into RDF, with a separate lexicon for each language using the lemon model (McCrae et al., 2011), and a translation set for each language pair[8].

3.4 Apertium

As Slovnyk mainly contains nouns and noun phrases, we automatically extracted verbs from the Apertium Russian-Ukrainian bilingual lexicon[9]. Apertium (Corbí Bellot et al., 2005) was an open-source rule-based Machine Translation platform, which therefore heavily relies on bilingual lexica and grammars. It is now supported by an online community[10]. This method enables to collect 1,215 different verbs, which were integrated into the Slovnyk Ukrainian dictionary.

3.5 Corpora

We use two corpora in our experiments. The first is the British National Corpus (BNC) (Burnard, 2007), a large reference corpus of British English (100 million words). We use the version that is available through PDEV and because it is annotated with pattern numbers.

The second corpus is OPUS, an aligned multilingual corpus containing various sources for 92 languages (Tiedemann, 2009). We focus on the Ukrainian-English pair which contains movie subtitles and technical software documentation (3.3 million words) made available through the SketchEngine query system (Kilgarriff et al., 2014).

4 WordNet senses as interlingual links

We present a cross lingual approach to establish links between lexical semantic resources (LSRs) and corpora.

Our approach is fairly standard in this respect as it aims to use WordNet (WN) as a multilingual index between languages. This approach requires two steps:

1. identify appropriate WN senses for each sense in each resource
2. link all entry pairs with a sense in common

The resulting translation pairs are the pairs which have a WN sense in common. This method can be applied to Open Multilingual WordNet. In this experiment we use COW, the Chinese Open

[5] `http://pdev.org.uk/#onto`
[6] `https://www.wiktionary.org/`
[7] `http://www.slovnyk.org/`
[8] `http://datahub.io/dataset/rdf-uk-es`
[9] `http://wiki.apertium.org/wiki/Russian_and_Ukrainian`
[10] `apertium.org`

WordNet, which provides links between Chinese words and WN senses (manually checked). The general workflow is illustrated in Figure 1

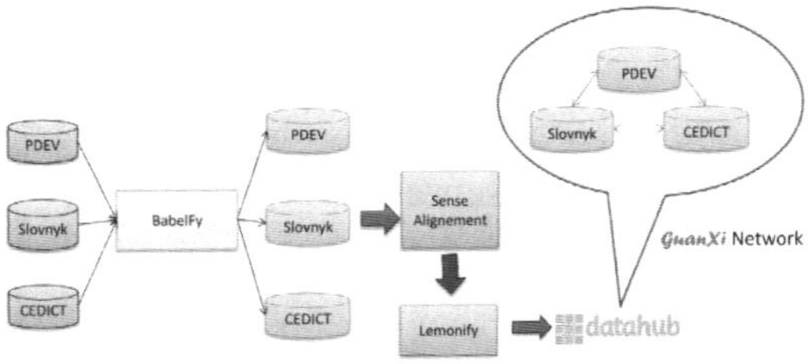

Figure 1: Approach workflow

4.1 Word Sense Disambiguation for Wordnet sense harvesting

PDEV is an isolated resource in the linked data cloud, so the links to WordNet need to be created. However it possesses its own sense-tagged corpus, which means that if the WordNet sense of the verb in one of these examples is correctly disambiguated, the pattern sense can be mapped to a WN sense. In order to do that, we mainly used the Babelfy API[11], which provides a disambiguation service that outputs a BabelNet sense for each content word. Since BabelNet builds on WordNet for verbs, the WN sense can straightforwardly be derived from the BabelNet sense. Thus all that is needed is an example of a sense from PDEV, in order for Babelfy to identify the relevant sense. This can be performed for any of the 271 languages covered by Babelfy.

However, this technique has its limits, since, as we discovered in our initial experiments, it is not possible to simply query Babelfy on any language and build bilingual lexica by collecting common senses. In fact, the languages targeted in the GuanXi network (Chinese and Ukrainian), have poor support and either need query pre-processing, or more lexical coverage. This is the reason why we made use of various data sources in combination: in order to link English with Chinese, we rely on the WN sense links provided in COW.

4.2 Beyond WordNet: Example-based sense mapping

For less resourced languages such as Ukrainian, which are not linked to WordNet, we propose an alternative example-based method, which consists in taking a non-English example and annotating relevant e.g. Ukrainian tokens with a pattern sense. Thus, we can harvest a sense for a Ukrainian verb (the pattern) and a link between English and Ukrainian (the translation) at the sense level.

The reason for using this approach is that we consider that PDEV patterns are very reliable representations of sentence meaning: as opposed to a standard definition or gloss, it specifies the contextual conditions of use in great detail, which is of great help to the annotator. Obviously, this will provide an incomplete picture of the language (since some senses which may be specific to a non-English language, with the consequence that finer-grained semantic preferences, may not be discovered with this technique), and cannot be used to identify translations which map to different parts of speech.

In this context, we can leverage examples from parallel corpora, which already provide translation candidates in context. This greatly decreases the workload on human annotation and provides a controlled framework for verb translation.

5 The Multilingual Corpus-Lexicon Model

5.1 Resources Types for Language Learning

The main type of resources that are connected in the GuanXi network are corpora, lexica and ontolgies (including taxonomies). Thanks to the concept of Linked Data, this network allows the extraction of multiple datasets resulting from different views on the network. Thus, it is possible to extract examples for senses, but also examples where a given semantic type is the subject of a verb, etc. Currently, only the verb token in the corpus example can be directly linked to lexical entries, but we intend to multiply annotations on examples in a semi-automatic way in order to enable the retrieval of other entities in each examples. Particularly we plan to include the Semeval 2015 dataset for Task 15[12], which includes annotations for 4,529 sentences, which can be straightforwardly mapped to both syntactic (syntactic relations) and semantic (semantic types) classes of PDEV-lemon.

We are particularly keen on using corpus examples because the end users of this resource, lan-

[11] `http://www.babelfy.org/`

[12] `alt.qcri.org/semeval2015/task15`

guage learners, need to work on/with real language use. PDEV provides the list of patterns that are most commonly used in English, i.e. those which a foreign speaker should learn in priority. In fact, it is possible to design a progressive learning curriculum, since PDEV provides percentages of uses of each pattern of each verb. PDEV also classifies examples according to whether they are normal pattern uses or creative and figurative uses. Selecting appropriate examples is therefore greatly facilitated by this prior massive manual work.

5.2 The GuanXi Framework

These resources can all be integrated into a data model. We use the lemon framework (McCrae et al., 2011) to represent the lexicons and the NIF model (Hellmann et al., 2013) to represent corpus data. Lemon has a relation for creating links between senses and examples but the example class is not structured. The ability to isolate a word from a sentence in order to refer to it, or to appropriately annotate a sentence part with links to features of an entry is instead provided by the NIF model. The main principle of lemon is to provide a model which enables the separation of lexical information from semantic information as provided in ontologies. The GuanXi network is connected to 8 ontologies and lexinfo[13]. Finally we use the translation[14] module described in (Gracia et al., 2014) as the translation framework for bilingual lexicons.

The resulting multilingual corpus-lexicon-ontology data model of the GuanXi is illustrated in Figure 2. As can be seen, we use a new relation *kwic* (Key Word In Context) to relate a particular token of a sentence in NIF representation with a lexical sense in a specific language. This link makes it possible to have a simple but powerful link between the corpus and the lexicon, without having to rely on external ontologies, in line with lemon principles. The translation set helps to connect various equivalent senses of words from different languages. The figure also shows the structure of PDEV verb entries and the links between the lexicon and the ontologies. It is worth noting that we only use the ontology part of FrameNet (the frame and frame elements), which is connected to a concept in the PDEV ontology.

[13] http://lexinfo.net/

[14] http://purl.org/net/translation.owl

6 Evaluation

6.1 Automatic evaluation through clustering similarity

The Babelfy system provides state of the art performance on Word Sense Disambiguation (WSD) (Moro et al., 2014). However, WSD systems can experience a significant drop in performance when evaluated on unseen data, and generally have very different results on different datasets.

Since the quality of the links of the GuanXi network depends on Babelfy's ability to identify the right BabelNet synset in context, we set up an experiment to automatically assess the quality of this disambiguation. Since each PDEV pattern is connected with a set of examples, we submitted these examples (to the maximum of 5 per pattern) for disambiguation to Babelfy and extracted the BabelNet synset.

In order to evaluate the quality of the mappings, we used the B-cubed definition of Precision and Recall, first used for coreference (Bagga and Baldwin, 1999) and later extended to cluster evaluation (Amigó et al., 2009). Both measures are averages of the precision and recall over all instances. To calculate the precision of each instance we count all correct pairs associated with this instance and divide by the number of actual pairs in the candidate cluster that the instance belongs to. Recall is computed by interchanging Gold and Candidate clusterings[15] (Eq. 1).

$$\begin{aligned} \mathrm{Precision_i} &= \frac{\mathrm{Pairs_i\ in\ Candidate\ found\ in\ Gold}}{\mathrm{Pairs_i\ in\ Candidate}} \\ \mathrm{Recall_i} &= \frac{\mathrm{Pairs_i\ in\ Gold\ found\ in\ Candidate}}{\mathrm{Pairs_i\ in\ Gold}} \end{aligned} \quad (1)$$

Table 1 compares Babelfy with standards WSD algorithms such as Simple Lesk (Lesk, 1986) or Adapted Lesk (Banerjee and Pedersen, 2002)[16], taking into account the full sentence. Every system beats the baseline, Baseline1, which consists in assigning all examples the same sense (i.e. without account of context). According to B-cubed F-score, Adapted Lesk provides clusterings which are the most similar to PDEV.

[15] A clustering is the set of clusters that a particular method outputs.

[16] This study uses the pywsd implementation; for more details, see (Tan, 2014)https://github.com/alvations/pywsd

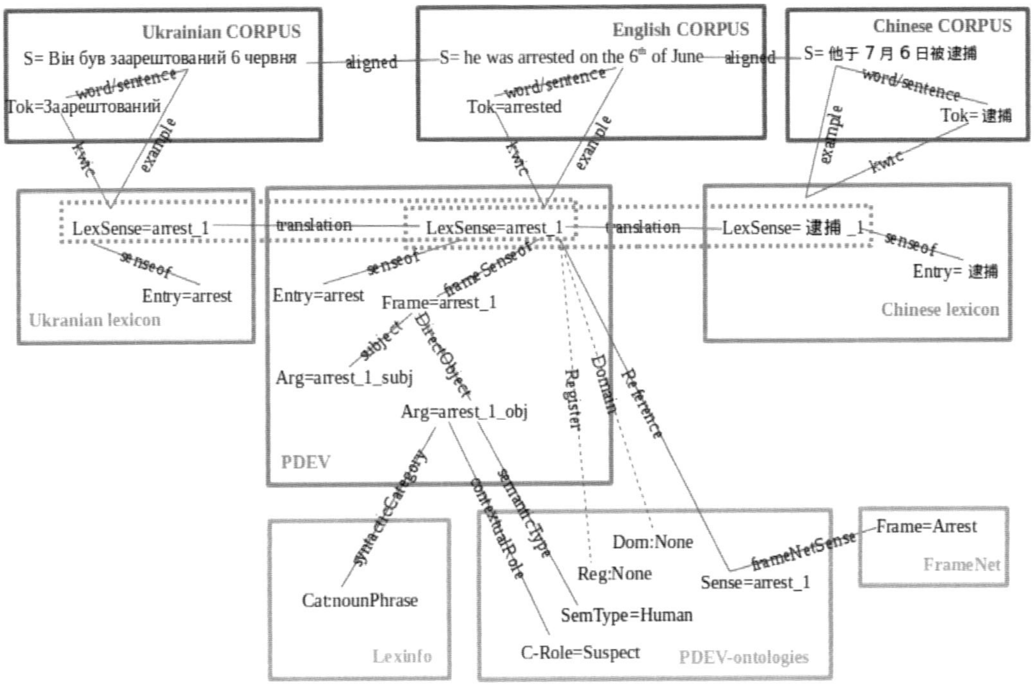

Figure 2: Guanxi Data Model

System	B^3 F-score
Cosine Lesk	0.470
Baseline1	0.472
Orig Lesk	0.579
Babelfy	0.639
Simple Lesk	0.655
Adapted Lesk	0.656

Table 1: Results for WSD on full sentence using B-cubed F-score.

Context	B^3 F-score
Size=1	0.633
Size=2	0.666
Size=3	0.668
Size=4	0.666
Size=5	0.662
Baseline1	0.472

Table 2: Optimising context size for Babelfy WSD using B-cubed F-score.

This evaluation calls for two warnings. First, evaluating the clusterings of two methods or resources tells in theory nothing about the quality of these clusters: a system might well cluster tokens identically to the reference but provide wrong pointers to WordNet definitions or senses. However in practice, assuming that good clusterings gives a strong indication of quality is a reasonable assumption.

The second warning is that clusters obtained from PDEV do not necessarily signal sense differences. Therefore the algorithm might well be correct in assigning to 2 different patterns, one and unique WordNet sense. However, as opposed to other clustering evaluation measures (see e.g. Measure Of Concordance (Pfitzner et al., 2009)), the B-cubed measure tends to attenuate the impact of this kind of cases.

We decided to use the Babelfy system for WSD, mainly because it returns BabelNet synsets, thereby providing access to many resources, and because previous evaluations have shown the effectiveness of the algorithm. So we proceeded to optimize the query system by identifying the best size for a query.

We submitted six sets of queries: queries which included one context word (on each side of the target word) in addition to the target word, but also two, three, four, and five context words, and the full example. Table 2 shows that the optimal size of context for Babelfy is 3 words on each side of the target word, and no benefit is obtained by taking into account more context; on the contrary, the performance tends to decrease, to the point that it is almost equivalent to a context size of 1.

6.2 Chinese manual evaluation

We generated a small corpus of examples for each PDEV pattern, with maximum 5 examples per pattern. This covered 4,532 patterns of 1,274 verbs. We used Babelfy with the best setup (+-/3 words) to get the WN synsets.

Out of 19,651 English queries, Babelfy returned links to WordNet except for 279 examples (NA), and 216 "null" WN senses (95 verbs, 88 nouns, 30 adj, and 3 adverbs), meaning a coverage rate of 97.5% (4,469 patterns for 1,240 verbs). With respect to null verb synsets, these are senses from the Wiktionary that have not been mapped to a WordNet synset. For example, *rewind* with the gloss *to wind (something) again*, also exists in WordNet with the gloss *rewind (wind (up) again) 'the mechanical watch needs rewinding every day'*. Example (1) illustrates a case of NA concerning verb *abduct*, which is probably due to a processing error or threshold on the Babelfy API.

(1) Police believe he died a few hours after he was abducted .

Our version of COW contains 80,010 word-synset pairs, covering 61,535 Chinese words and 42,315 English synsets. Out of these, 1,214 COW different links to WN overlapped with those obtained with Babelfy. 10,796 examples (55%) could be matched with a common WN synset, covering 2,918 patterns (65%) for 807 entries (65%).

We then proceeded to evaluate the accuracy of the English-Chinese sense links by assessing manually for each example whether the Chinese translation could be substituted to the English verb in a translation of the whole sentence into Chinese. To simplify the task, we reduced the data in the following two ways:

- Only one Chinese word was used as a translation of a synset (for example 鼓动, 挑起, and 煽动all map to 02585050-v glossed as "try to stir up public opinion", according to COW), initially randomly selected (we selected only 鼓动, when Babelfy disambiguated a given verb use as 02585050-v).
- Redundant examples were removed from the evaluation on the grounds that because they are all examples of the same pattern, the validity of one translation should be valid for all other examples.

The results show that 1,598 (4,872 over the whole set of examples) examples were correct, and 2,079 were wrong (5,920). This covers 743 verbs and 869 Chinese words for 1,468 PDEV patterns/senses and 959 WN synsets.

The benefits of this method are to get a fine-grained evaluation of sense links between Chinese words and WordNet senses based on examples. Errors can either be explained by a wrong mapping in COW, but most realistically, the experience of the Chinese annotator is that Chinese translations in COW are context-insensitive, and are only wrong in that sense. This is generally a consequence of the concept of synset which groups words sharing similar meanings, but where members of the synset cannot strictly be substituted in every context (there are no exact synonyms in natural languages).

An example-based approach provides the missing piece of the puzzle. Because examples are linked to patterns, we can also transfer the semantic structures (arguments) from English to Chinese, in order to draft automatically entries for Chinese words as part of a multilingual pattern dictionary. For example, 鼓动was correctly found to link to the second pattern of *agitate*, and we can therefore suggest that when this Chinese verb has [[Anything]] as subject and either [[Human]], [[Institution]] or [[Animal]] as direct object, it means "[[Anything]] makes [[Human | Institution | Animal]] feel anxious, alarmed, or nervous"as in "The Admiralty was sorely agitated by the shipwrights' custom of taking 'chips'."

Last but not least, this method also allows to collect more than one WN sense for a given pattern sense. Thus whenever two patterns point to the same synset, it entails that they are semantically similar, and that PDEV is making a distinction where WordNet isn't, and vice versa. Thus, both patterns of verb *fidget* map to the same WN synset 02058448-v "move restlessly", but PDEV makes a distinction between fidgeting with a [[Physical Object]] and the intransitive use. This method also enables to harvest similarities between patterns belonging to different verbs such as *cooling* and *chilling* in the spirit of WN synsets.

6.3 Ukrainian manual study

We attempted to use the Babelfy disambiguation system for Ukrainian. However, Ukrainian is a less resourced language, and Babelfy returned very few hits, probably because of the limited success or availability of tokenization, part of speech tagging tools, as well as the low coverage of existing lexical resources for Ukrainian. We submitted 20 sentences and only two Ukrainian verbs returned results, but were translated to nouns.

However, we proceeded to evaluate whether parallel resources could reliably be used by lexicographers to automatically draft bilingual dictionaries, and in our case, to align PDEV to Ukrainian. We used the SketchEngine (Kilgarriff et al., 2014) to extract verbs from the OPUS aligned corpus and presented the lexicographer with the Ukrainian word and the sentence pair. The lexicographer's task was to identify the word in the English sentence which translated the Ukrainian verb, if any, and look up in PDEV if a pattern number could be matched.

The evaluation revealed that, out of 100 examples, 36 were problematic:

- 17 cases were pre-processing issues where no English sentence was presented to the user. The lexicographer translated and aligned them to PDEV but could not evaluate the English alignment.
- 9 verbs did not have a direct equivalent in the English translation.
- 6 verbs had problematic English translations, including not appropriate, bad, or incorrect translations. These were corrected and mapped to PDEV.

Thus 64% of examples could be used to link Ukrainian with English. However, only 17% of examples (10% without human intervention) matched an existing PDEV entry, which accounts for 63 verbs not being described yet in PDEV. An example of a satisfactory link is illustrated in examples (2a) and (2b).

(2a) Якщо буде позначено цей пункт , К3б не буде **висувати** лоток з носієм відразу після завершення запису .

(2b) If this option is checked K3b will not **eject** the medium once the burn process finishes .

The pattern illustrated is eject 4 (see Table 3).

Pattern [[Machine]] ejects [[Artifact]]	
Implicatures [[Machine]] pushes out [[Artifact]] *This is generally a case of a disc or other hardware being ejected by a computer or other technological device*	

Table 3: PDEV pattern 4 of eject

7 Conclusion and Future Work

This paper reports on the evaluation of current linked data solutions to build a multilingual network, which integrates lexicons, ontologies, and corpora to serve Language Learning applications, especially in the process of building learning materials and activities. The paper proposes a data model for the network, in which knowledge can be conveyed from one resource to another, from one language to another. This is particularly useful for language learning, as several views on the data can be created for different audiences or different language topics (meaning, grammar, spelling, etc.). This paper focuses on sense linking for multilingual resources (English, Chinese, and Ukrainian) and proposes several methods to achieve this goal, depending on available resources. Because quality is an essential feature of such an application, the paper runs several evaluations of existing resources and state-of-the-art NLP and WSD systems. The evaluations are quite pessimistic as sense linking success is hindered by errors introduced at various stages, or insufficient coverage of lexical resources.

Extracting reliable links, however, is a major issue in Linguistic Linked Data, and there are various other methods than the ones presented in this paper to achieve it. We are particularly interested in evaluating distributional thesauri automatically constructed from corpora to identify sense candidates, as well as semi-supervised methods, where a few translated examples are provided as seeds to a bootstrapping algorithm.

Perspectives also include evaluating PDEV pattern transfers to languages such as Ukrainian and Chinese, and particularly enable an evaluation of cross-lingual verb semantic preferences. With a view on the language learning application, we intend to evaluate how images and other media can be collected and sense-linked to our network, much like what BabelNet proposes.

References

Eneko Agirre and Aitor Soroa. 2009. Personalizing pagerank for word sense disambiguation. In *Proceedings of the 12th Conference of the European Chapter of the Association for Computational Linguistics*, pages 33–41. Association for Computational Linguistics.

Enrique Amigó, Julio Gonzalo, Javier Artiles, and Felisa Verdejo. 2009. A comparison of extrinsic clustering evaluation metrics based on formal constraints. *Information Retrieval*, 12(4):461–486.

Amit Bagga and Breck Baldwin. 1999. Cross-document event coreference: Annotations, experiments, and observations. In *Proceedings of the Workshop on Coreference and its Applications*, pages 1–8.

Vìt Baisa, Jane Bradbury, Silvie Cinková, Ismaïl El Maarouf, Patrick Hanks, Adam Kilgarriff, and Octavian Popescu. 2015. Semeval-2015 task 15: A cpa dictionary-entry-building task. In *Proceedings of the 9th International Workshop on Semantic Evaluation (SemEval 2015)*, Denver, Co, USA.

Satanjeev Banerjee and Ted Pedersen. 2002. An adapted lesk algorithm for word sense disambiguation using wordnet. In *Computational linguistics and intelligent text processing*, pages 136–145. Springer.

Francis Bond and Ryan Foster. 2013. Linking and extending an open multilingual wordnet. In *ACL (1)*, pages 1352–1362.

Francis Bond and Kyonghee Paik. 2012. A survey of wordnets and their licenses. In *Proceedings of the 6th International Global WordNet Conference*, pages 64–71.

Lou Burnard. 2007. Reference guide for the british national corpus (xml edition), 2007. *URL http://www. natcorp. ox. ac. uk/XMLedition/URG*.

Antonio Miguel Corbí Bellot, Mikel L Forcada Zubizarreta, Sergio Ortiz Rojas, Juan Antonio Pérez Ortiz, Gema Ramírez Sánchez, Felipe Sánchez Martínez, Iñaki Alegría Loinaz, Aingeru Mayor Martínez, Kepa Sarasola Gabiola, et al. 2005. An open-source shallow-transfer machine translation engine for the romance languages of spain. In *European Association for Machine Translation*.

Ismail El Maarouf, Jane Bradbury, and Patrick Hanks. 2014. Pdev-lemon: a linked data implementation of the pattern dictionary of english verbs based on the lemon model. In *Proceedings of the 3rd Workshop on Linked Data in Linguistics (LDL): Multilingual Knowledge Resources and Natural Language Processing at the Ninth International Conference on Language Resources and Evaluation (LREC'14)*, Reykjavik, Iceland.

Charles J. Fillmore. 1985. Frames and the semantics of understanding. *Quaderni di Semantica*, 6(2):222–254.

Jorge Gracia, Elena Montiel-Ponsoda, Daniel Vila-Suero, and Guadalupe Aguado-de-Cea. 2014. Enabling language resources to expose translations as linked data on the web. In *Proceedings of the Ninth International Conference on Language Resources and Evaluation (LREC-2014), Reykjavik, Iceland, May 26-31, 2014.*, pages 409–413.

Iryna Gurevych, Judith Eckle-Kohler, Silvana Hartmann, Michael Matuschek, Christian M Meyer, and Christian Wirth. 2012. Uby: A large-scale unified lexical-semantic resource based on lmf. In *Proceedings of the 13th Conference of the European Chapter of the Association for Computational Linguistics*, pages 580–590. Association for Computational Linguistics.

Patrick Hanks and James Pustejovsky. 2005. A pattern dictionary for natural language processing. *Revue Française de linguistique appliquée*, 10:2.

Patrick Hanks. 2012. How people use words to make meanings: Semantic types meet valencies. In A. Boulton and J. Thomas, editors, *Input, Process and Product: Developments in Teaching and Language Corpora*, pages 54–69. Masaryk University Press, Brno.

Patrick Hanks. 2013. *Lexical Analysis: Norms and Exploitations*. MIT Press, Cambridge, MA.

Sebastian Hellmann, Jens Lehmann, Sören Auer, and Martin Brümmer. 2013. Integrating nlp using linked data. In *The Semantic Web–ISWC 2013*, pages 98–113. Springer.

Adam Kilgarriff and Martha Palmer. 2000. Introduction to the special issue on senseval. *Computers and the Humanities*, 34:1–2.

Adam Kilgarriff, Vít Baisa, Jan Bušta, Miloš Jakubíček, Vojtěch Kovář, Jan Michelfeit, Pavel Rychlý, and Vít Suchomel. 2014. The sketch engine: ten years on. *Lexicography*, 1(1):7–36.

Michael Lesk. 1986. Automatic sense disambiguation using machine readable dictionaries: How to tell a pine cone from an ice cream cone. In *Proceedings of the 5th Annual International Conference on Systems Documentation*, SIGDOC '86, pages 24–26, New York, NY, USA. ACM.

Michael Matuschek and Iryna Gurevych. 2013. Dijkstra-wsa: A graph-based approach to word sense alignment. *Transactions of the Association for Computational Linguistics*, 1:151–164.

John McCrae, Dennis Spohr, and Philipp Cimiano. 2011. Linking lexical resources and ontologies on the semantic web with lemon. In *Proceedings of the 8th Extended Semantic Web Conference on The Semantic Web: Research and Applications - Volume*

Part I, ESWC'11, pages 245–259, Berlin, Heidelberg. Springer-Verlag.

Rada Mihalcea. 2005. Unsupervised large-vocabulary word sense disambiguation with graph-based algorithms for sequence data labeling. In *Proceedings of the Conference on Human Language Technology and Empirical Methods in Natural Language Processing*, HLT '05, pages 411–418, Stroudsburg, PA, USA. Association for Computational Linguistics.

Andrea Moro, Alessandro Raganato, and Roberto Navigli. 2014. Entity linking meets word sense disambiguation: A unified approach. *Transactions of the Association for Computational Linguistics*, 2:231–244.

Roberto Navigli and Simone Paolo Ponzetto. 2012. BabelNet: The automatic construction, evaluation and application of a wide-coverage multilingual semantic network. *Artificial Intelligence*, 193:217–250.

Roberto Navigli. 2009. Word sense disambiguation: A survey. *ACM Comput. Surv.*, 41(2):10:1–10:69, February.

Elisabeth Niemann and Iryna Gurevych. 2011. The people's web meets linguistic knowledge: Automatic sense alignment of wikipedia and wordnet. In *Proceedings of the 9th International Conference on Computational Semantics*, pages 205–214, Singapore, January.

Darius Pfitzner, Richard Leibbrandt, and David Powers. 2009. Characterization and evaluation of similarity measures for pairs of clusterings. *Knowledge Information Systems*, 19(3):361–394.

Gilles Sérasset. 2012. Dbnary: Wiktionary as a LMF based Multilingual RDF network. In *Language Resources and Evaluation Conference, LREC 2012*, Istanbul, Turkey, May. Nicoletta Calzolari and Khalid Choukri and Thierry Declerck and Mehmet Uğur Doğan and Bente Maegaard and Joseph Mariani and Jan Odijk and Stelios Piperidis.

Liling Tan. 2014. Pywsd: Python implementations of word sense disambiguation (wsd) technologies [software]. https://github.com/alvations/pywsd.

Jörg Tiedemann. 2009. News from opus-a collection of multilingual parallel corpora with tools and interfaces. In *Recent advances in natural language processing*, volume 5, pages 237–248.

Shan Wang and Francis Bond. 2013. Building the chinese open wordnet (cow): Starting from core synsets. In *Sixth International Joint Conference on Natural Language Processing*, page 10. Citeseer.

Renjie Xu, Zhiqiang Gao, Yingji Pan, Yuzhong Qu, and Zhisheng Huang. 2008. An integrated approach for automatic construction of bilingual chinese-english wordnet. In *Proceedings of the 3rd Asian Semantic Web Conference on The Semantic Web*, ASWC '08, pages 302–314, Berlin, Heidelberg. Springer-Verlag.

Author Index

Association for Computational Linguistics
209 N. Eighth Street
Stroudsburg, Pennsylvania 18360

ISBN 978-1-5108-1783-8

CURRAN ASSOCIATES INC.
proceedings.com

ASPRS Annual Conference 2020

ISPRS Archives Volume XLIV-M-2-2020,2020

Online
22 – 26 June 2020

information from imagery